The Extra Mile

The Extra Mile

A *Twenty-first-century Pilgrimage*

PETER STANFORD

continuum

Published by the Continuum International Publishing Group Ltd
The Tower Building, 11 York Road, London SE1 7NX
80 Maiden Lane, Suite 704, New York NY 10038

www.continuumbooks.com

Copyright © Peter Stanford, 2010

Quotations from 'Pilgrimages' from *Frequencies* (1978) and 'Counterpoint' (1990) by R. S. Thomas, © Kunjana Thomas. Used by permission.

First published 2010

British Library Cataloguing-in-Publication Data
A catalogue record for this book is available from the British Library.

ISBN: 978–0–8264–3404–3

Designed and typeset by Kenneth Burnley, Wirral, Cheshire
Printed and bound by the MPG Books Group

Contents

Introduction   vii

1   Stonehenge   1

2   Bardsey Island   24

3   The Wells of Derbyshire   50

4   Walsingham   74

5   Holywell   99

6   Iona   129

7   Lindisfarne   154

8   Glastonbury   179

Acknowledgements   201

To Kit and Orla –

my companions on my travels

Introduction

Waterden church stands alone in the middle of a field. There isn't even a path up to it, just a gap in the hedgerow and a trail across the grass. It is a Norfolk village church without a village. Parts of its just-about-watertight fabric are believed to date back to the Domesday Book of 1086 which makes mention of a church at Waterden, but whatever parish it served then or since moved away long ago. The former rectory in incongruous Victorian Gothic stands well apart from it, all but hidden behind a screen of trees. Otherwise there is not a single building in sight, only farmland rolling down the hill towards the track of an old Roman road (this part of north Norfolk belies the county's reputation for being flat), big skies and wild flowers in the overgrown graveyard.

Whenever I am in the vicinity of Waterden, I make a pilgrimage there. I use the word 'pilgrimage' deliberately. This is not just a ramble into the countryside, or the opportunity to inflict on my children (who often come along) a lecture on Jesus or ecclesiastical architecture. Waterden is, for me, a sacred spot; a verdict I reached instinctively long before I tried to analyse what it really meant.

When I did, I came up with three factors. First, what draws me back time and again is the silence. I did once attend a magical Christmas Eve service, when candlelight illuminated the frosty breath of singers (there's no electricity and no heating), but otherwise I've never met anyone else there, or thereabouts, though a notice in the porch refers to the occasional Evensong, and the yellowing visitors' book shows signs of life.

Then there is the mystery. What happened to the parish? To the Money-Hills whose graves are below the chancel floor? North Norfolk is full of once-thriving villages that have been taken over by second-homers and lie deserted during the week and in winter, but here at Waterden even the houses have gone. And the fabric of the church itself belies interpretation. Though small, it contains jumbled-up fragments of Saxon, Norman and Early English styles, as well as seventeenth-century mullions. It's like an architectural Rubik's cube. There is also the outline of a lost south aisle (to accommodate whom?), numerous blocked-up windows, and the ruins of a bell tower with walls that are surely too thin ever to have supported even a roof. Which may be why it collapsed. Not that anyone would have been here to notice.

You could reasonably argue that mystery and silence can be found in many places that would not merit the label 'sacred'. What clinches it for me, though, is that when about and around this hauntingly beautiful church, I am aware of an unformed presence, hovering at the edge of my senses. It is nothing as crass as ghosts, or unquiet spirits, wandering the graveyard, but just as illogical in our sceptical, scientific and secular age. The complete disconnection of Waterden with the modern world gives me a sense when here of walking in the footsteps of people of faith in ages past, of joining a human chain that draws me towards . . . well, towards their faith. It is, I accept, a hard one to put into words without sounding pious.

Too many religiously minded individuals, not all of them clerics, try repeatedly to 'prove' the existence of God. It is, as far as I can see, a futile exercise. God is beyond proof. That is the point of faith. It is implied in the very word, certainly in the way I use it.

Attempting, week in, week out, to provide 'evidence' that there is a God has the opposite effect to what is intended by these no doubt sincere preachers. It turns off more people than it attracts. It is one of the reasons why there has been such an exodus of late from the mainstream Christian churches. The time-honoured 'proofs' no longer wash.

Yet that doesn't mean, as is sometimes suggested, that religion itself no longer has a purpose, or indeed a pull. People may be put off by the dogmatism and introspection of religious institutions. They may be more ready than ever before to subscribe uncritically to the assertion that religion simply causes wars and conflicts. But that does not mean that they have ceased to yearn for there to be something other, something beyond the narrow confines of the here and now, of this life, of the consumerism, of the relativist values of this world, of its rough and random justice. How, though, to explore that yearning, when to enter a church, mosque, temple or synagogue is – in their minds at least – to side with one camp or another, and to invite being lectured and judged?

A survey in 2009 by Christian Research showed that, as a result of the global economic downturn, three-quarters of the population of Britain had been prompted to reassess their core values. The brutal unveiling in many lives of the shortcomings of capitalism and materialism in terms of homes and jobs lost had caused them to reconsider the alternatives. High on any list of such options would be religions with their shared ethic of justice, equality and concern for the marginalized. Yet, Christian Research reported, only three per cent of these 'non-religious seekers' had contemplated going to a church. Only one per cent had actually given it a try, and none of them was planning to repeat the experience.

Where else then might they look? Or where are they looking? Christian Research mentions volunteering and hobbies. Other sources point to a surge in popularity of retreat centres or 'taster' weekends and weeks at monasteries. The sales success of Sara Maitland's recent *Book of Silence*, an account of her embracing the life of a hermit in rural Galloway, placed in the context of the long history within religions of rejecting the world, is surely another indicator that something, somewhere, is moving.

Waterden church set me off thinking about gauging that movement in sacred spots, the places where spirituality has been concentrated in ages past, and where traces of it may remain still. Usually they are called holy places, but what exactly does 'holy' mean? This is how the writer and poet, William Anderson, put it in a 1983 survey of the sacred landscape of Britain: 'When we speak of a place as being holy, we say something about its innate and acquired atmosphere, its emotional nature.' It is good, as far as it goes, but somehow sounds too passive, that we go to these holy places with no baggage and they work their magic on us. Surely it is a two-way process? We project our longings onto them too.

I listened recently to the 92-year-old former Chancellor of the Exchequer, Denis Healey, on BBC Radio 4's *Desert Island Discs*, saying that at his great age he reads only poetry. I knew at once what he meant. Poetry has that knack of saying eloquently what too often goes unsaid – because it is so hard to define – in the books and films and blogs and newspaper columns that swamp us. So I turn unapologetically to T. S. Eliot and *The Four Quartets* to express this urge towards sacred spots/holy places so much better than I could ever do. 'Little Gidding' was inspired by Eliot's 1936 visit to the church and buildings in Huntingdonshire that housed a now-defunct seventeenth-century high-minded Anglican community.

> If you came this way,
> Taking any route, starting from anywhere,
> At any time or at any season,
> It would always be the same: you would have to put off
> Sense and notion. You are not here to verify,
> Instruct yourself, or inform curiosity
> Or carry report. You are here to kneel
> Where prayer has been valid. And prayer is more
> Than an order of words, the conscious occupation
> Of the praying mind, or the sound of the voice praying.
> And what the dead had no speech for, when living,
> They can tell you, being dead: the communication
> Of the dead is tongued with fire beyond the language of
>   the living.
> Here, the intersection of the timeless moment
> Is England and nowhere. Never and always.

That idea of people setting off, not to verify but simply to kneel where prayer was once valid, is the starting point for this book and the pilgrimage it describes. The notion of aspects of the landscape giving us an insight into the creator God is, of course, a cliché. Sunrise, sunset, mountains, sea, rivers, great cathedrals, fields of corn blowing in the breeze, have all been invoked in prayers and hymns as lifting the veil on God's proximity. Much as we are taught to sneer at and avoid the cliché, it is worth remembering that the reason certain ideas and images become clichés in the first place is precisely because they hit upon a truth that many recognize. The problems come when the cliché is repeated too emphatically. So, as one of those rare clerics who is also a scientist remarked recently, the wonder of the universe does not prove God, but it certainly poses questions.

Britain has arguably as many holy places per square mile as any other island in the world. Some of these locations where heaven and earth are said to have touched have been hallowed by an unbroken tradition of prayer going back millennia. Others have a more fragmented story and testify to the changing religious climate here over the centuries. Some are well known, others less so. Some continue to operate as shrines, others simply as historical places of interest. Most have, woven into their legend, an element of unsolved mystery.

What they all have in common, though, as I discovered as I worked my way round them, is that something is stirring there. Numbers of visitors in most are up, as are numbers of visitors who come not just as tourists, or to sample a slice of the past, but to participate. These are non-religious seekers, curious as to whether the history of witness to faith at these holy places has anything to say to current times and current concerns. So that search for something other than the promises of money and material plenty that have been shown so hollow can be detected at these ancient sites; but it is a story that is below the radar of news headlines, and certainly doesn't register in the church-going statistics as they tumble remorselessly in most denominations.

To investigate it, I became convinced I needed to go the extra mile to uncover what these seekers were finding at sacred spots. Pilgrimage has always carried connotations of hard physical slog, and most of the places featured in this journey were indeed hard to get to. Several were to be found on islands where the tides managed to introduce an element of risk as to whether I would ever arrive on their shores safely. Or be able to leave. And then there were my inhibitions to overcome. It has become easier in the current climate to keep quiet about faith if you have one, especially if you want to explore it. As Tony Blair remarked, on becoming a Catholic after resigning as Prime Minister, he hadn't spoken about God when in office in case people assumed he was a 'nutter'. So to join a pilgrimage, to stand at Stonehenge at dawn with Druids in extraordinary costumes while lorry-drivers on the nearby roads looked on and tooted their horns in laughter, or to join a procession carrying a cross over the mud-flats to Lindisfarne with onlookers staring in blank incomprehension, requires if not courage, then at least a willingness to risk going against the cultural grain.

The eight locations covered in this book are very much a personal selection. There were many others that would have served equally well: the shrine church of the fourteenth-century mystic, Julian of Norwich; the restored sections of the ancient Canterbury Pilgrims' Way, immortalized by Geoffrey Chaucer in his *Canterbury Tales* in the fourteenth century; 'Cerne Man', the giant figure cut out of a chalky hillside in Dorset, and a site of fertility rites dating back to Roman times and perhaps beyond; Pennant Melangell, in rural Montgomeryshire, a pre-Reformation place of pilgrimage where the twelfth-century shrine was later buried in the walls and only uncovered at the end of the last century; or the sea caves of Fife, with their ancient devotional carvings in the rock.

Those that made it onto my itinerary recommended themselves for several reasons beyond mere whim. One was that, put together, their individual stories more or less made up a snapshot of the history of faith in Britain, something increasingly lost as anything religious is pushed to the margins of the curriculum. Some have indeed played their part in key moments of that history.

I tried to time my arrival to coincide with the presence of pilgrimages, festivals, missions and exhibitions because they seemed to offer a chance to listen to the people who were visiting, to explore with them the spiritual map that had brought them there. The chapters of this book follow the chronology of my visits. They start with the summer solstice at Stonehenge in June 2008 and end with Beltane celebrations in Glastonbury in May 2009, almost a full liturgical cycle.

For the most part I have tried to observe and describe the various ceremonies I attended, rather than participate in them. This is not, I should say as emphatically as I can, a book that has any ambitions to hold up any one faith alternative above another. Evangelizing has never been my bag. I am happy to be as I wish to be and show the same respect for others' convictions that I would want them to show mine. That is, after all, the so-called 'golden rule' at the heart of all religions. But I have never been that good at boundaries and, on occasion, as you will read, I have stepped over the line and joined in with a ceremony. My motivation was not to make any sort of commitment to what was going on, or even to put the claims being made for it to the test, but rather to follow the logic of pilgrimage, that it requires an input, an openness, and even a childlike curiosity.

One of my first jobs was at the *Catholic Herald* newspaper. A weekly task was to sub-edit the then editor's column, called 'People and Places'. It was not a sought-after role, but the formula People and Places has kept coming back to me throughout this journey. Each chapter is a combination of the two components. The exact balance depends on how my time at the particular location panned out, but this is as much an account of other pilgrims as it is of history, or my reflections. In some spots, the people spoke to me more than the location. In others it was the other way round.

Inevitably, our backgrounds shape how we react to what we

encounter, so I should be upfront about my own starting point. I am not a non-religious seeker, to use the jargon. I did well enough subbing 'People and Places' columns to end up as editor of the *Catholic Herald* for four years in the late 1980s and early 1990s, and thereafter have continued to write, talk and broadcast on (among other things) the role of religion in our society, and sometimes specifically on Catholicism, the faith of my upbringing and still my given denominational attachment.

One of the benefits of that work over two decades is that it has exposed me to many other creeds and spiritual approaches, from animists in Angola and Candomble in Brazil, through to fundamentalist Islam in the East End of London. While I continue, in my own religious search, to work with what I was given – i.e. Catholicism – I hope that this exposure means my eyes are not too narrowly focused. Indeed, acutely aware as I am of the many institutional shortcomings of Catholicism, I could never absolutely rule out the possibility of seeking a transfer, though nothing has come my way thus far that appears, in an institutional sense, any less flawed. However, the search for spirituality, for the divine, for transcendence, that sense of life penetrated by the eternal, that there is more to this life than shows up under microscopes, is not limited by the confines of denominations, certainly not in relation to holy places that have been claimed by a procession of churches and cults down the ages.

The logic of most faiths is that, in everyday life, the sacred is always just beyond our reach. We aspire, we hope, we yearn, we want to believe, but it escapes our grasp. Yet some report touching it, albeit fleetingly, in moments of transcendence in their lives. They arrive we know not when. For me it was on my mother's deathbed when, heavily sedated, from out of nowhere she began singing. She had never been much of a singer, but now her voice was strong and pure. 'It's the drugs,' the nurse told me, but if drugs could turn a woman who tended to mouth the words of songs in church into Lesley Garrett, then we would all be taking them.

Holy places, too, carry with them that potential of transcendence, stepping out of time and out of character. And pilgrimages, I came to realize on my travels, are not just walking tourism. There is an interplay going on between the inner and the outer. For their premise is that the sacred is not always absolutely immaterial. The pilgrimage is, after all, seeking the spiritual through something material – the stories of those who have passed along the same road before, or straightforward, tangible geography and buildings. That is why pilgrims head for Bethlehem – to stand in the place where Jesus was born. Moreover, the very act of going on pilgrimage might be seen as making the body do what the soul desires, giving those spiritual yearnings a practical, material basis. In so doing, it runs counter to the powerful idea, found in most mainstream religions, that the spiritual is within us, and therefore utterly immaterial, rather than in the world, but that is so daunting. We don't know where to start. We do know, however, how to walk, how to go from here to there.

So was I swept up or swept away in any of the places I went to? In Tolstoy's *War and Peace*, Princess Marya Bolkonskoya feeds the Russian pilgrims who pass by her home. 'Often as she listened to the pilgrims' tales she was so fired by their simple speech, natural to them, but to her full of deep meaning, that several times she was on the point of abandoning everything and running away from home.' Did I follow her example? You will have to read on to find out.

1

Stonehenge

I single to Stonehenge, over the plain and some prodigious
great hills . . . came thither, and find them as prodigious as
any tales I ever heard of them, and worth going this journey
to see.

Samuel Pepys (1668)

There is a smoky, reddish glow to the dark grey sky outside the
car window as we head over Salisbury Plain. It doesn't look
like the middle of the night. Or anything like I imagine the
middle of the night to be in the depths of countryside – namely
a bluey-black blanket that smothers every detail, including
hands held directly in front of faces. Yet my watch is unam-
biguous. It is 3.30 a.m. This is night time.

My companions on this journey are old hands at these early
hours. They're Druids, worshippers at the shrine of nature and
its awesome powers, and therefore regular nocturnal pilgrims
on the solstices and equinoxes, connoisseurs of sunrises and
sunsets. 'Shouldn't it still be dark?' I ask, childlike, but too dis-
concerted to keep quiet any longer. What if we have set off too
late and are going to miss the sunrise at Stonehenge on Old
Midsummer's Day?

'Don't worry,' says Phil, also known as Bear, his craft
name, the rough equivalent among pagans of the saints'
names Christians take on at confirmation. Phil is a computer
programmer in his late thirties. He's a loner, he confides, not
a joiner of things. He is staring intently at the road ahead,
his brow creased under a Crocodile Dundee hat. 'We've cut
it fine a few times,' he admits, sitting ever further forward in

the driving seat, taking corners on the empty road slightly too fast for comfort, 'but sun-up isn't until 4.48 today.'

The road ducks in and out of the valley of the Avon – the Wiltshire Avon that flows southwards into the English Channel. As we climb up from among the willow and sedge that line its banks, Salisbury Plain is covered with a white mist that hovers just above the fields. It makes me feel as if I am looking out of an aircraft window. 'It all used to be ancient forest here,' explains Theo, Phil's wife, a charity worker. They are physical opposites – he's tall, craggy, held-in; she's smaller, rounder, and with dancing, engaging eyes. She's also known as Changeling – from a time, she explains, before she found Druidry, when her spiritual quest was directing her towards faeries. She is perched on the back seat in a wrap-round purple cape and flowing full-length skirt. 'Trees are very important to Druids – the ancient British trees like ash, oak and blackthorn.'

'But, some people dispute that it was still a forest when Stonehenge was built,' Phil interjects. Another contrast: he is precise where Theo is elaborate. She fills the silences. He lets them be. I'm more like Theo and, anyway, these are the first of Britain's estimated 10,000 Druids I've ever knowingly met, so I have enough curiosity to avoid any lulls in the conversation. Do people treat you differently when you tell them you are Druids? 'Not generally,' reflects Theo. 'The people I work with know if I'm taking a day off for a Druid meeting or ceremony.' She pauses. 'But in my last job a few odd things were said. And according to others I have been fortunate.'

Druids do seem to have a bit of an image problem. In the popular imagination, they are almost indistinguishable from witches and the Wicker Man of Christopher Lee's cult 1973 horror flick. Eighteenth-century writers regularly charged them with offering human sacrifice, and that mud is still sticking. 'For some Druids', Theo goes on, 'there is the equivalent of "coming out", admitting to colleagues and family that they are Druids.'

Druidry is a belief system based not on a book or a written text, but claims roots in an ancient and instinctive connection to the earth and to pagan practices that date back beyond Christianity (though this is disputed – a subject we will return to). 'What I like about it,' muses Theo, ignoring the bumps in the road as she sways from side to side as we hurl round corners, 'is that it is broad and tolerant. It doesn't do that Christian thing of saying it is a better way than any other. It is just one way that works for me. And it complements other parts of my life – like the yoga I've started doing.'

If forests there once were up here, they were cleared many centuries ago, leaving the undulating plateau of Salisbury Plain as featureless coarse grassland, much of it used today as an army training base. 'You should be able to see it any minute now,' says Phil. Theo tries to redirect my anxiety about arriving late onto the weather. 'The idea of hope', she says soothingly, 'is always a part of our journeys. We always come in the hope of seeing the sunrise, but it could rain or be obscured by cloud. Hope is essential with nature ceremonies because you never quite know what is going to happen weather-wise. That's why our rituals are also unpredictable. We adapt to the conditions we find.'

*   *   *

In the 1970s and 1980s, dawn on the longest day, 21 June, became the cue for a mass invasion of Stonehenge by various hippies, junkies, bikers, travellers, New Agers and assorted seekers, all hanging loose under the banner of a 'Free Festival'. It grew in size, disorder and disorientation until it all came to a sticky end in 1985 with the 'Battle of the Bean-field', when police blocked off access to the stones. Legal arguments ensued until, in a landmark House of Lords ruling of 1999, the site's owners, English Heritage, agreed that on certain prearranged dates and in negotiation with a 'round table' – a users' committee on which Theo sits – limited access would once again be permitted. It was quite a conces-sion, since for the rest of the year the heart of Stonehenge, a World Heritage Site, is isolated beyond the rope barriers to protect the stones from the threat of further wear and tear, also known as tourists.

Some 30,000 seekers had turned up this year on 21 June – three days ago – to mark the solstice with a great big party; but this morning's ritual, Theo and Phil explain, will be something much more spiritual and exclusive, a chance for true believers to cleanse and bring peace to Stonehenge, which they regard as an ancient temple, after the recent invasion by the hoi-polloi. Attendance is strictly by ticket only and is restricted to 200. The Druid Network, a loose association that represents one part of the many-winged family of British Druids, handles admission on a democratic first come, first served basis. I'm being allowed in as Theo and Phil's guest.

Druids like using phrases drawn from what they call 'old British', based loosely on Celtic nomenclature (though this is disputed by some academics). So they are calling today Alban Hefin – in addition to Old Midsummer's Day – while the gathering at Stonehenge is a Gorsedd of Bards of Cor Gawr – roughly, a meeting of mighty poets.

It looks more like a gathering of the teaching staff from Harry Potter's Hogwarts as we pull into the car park of the Visitor Centre. The figures moving round in the dry ice of the pre-dawn haze could belong to any epoch, save perhaps the first decade of the twenty-first century. Cloaks are the uniform of choice, floor-length, hooded and invariably with flared sleeves. There is plenty of colour variation, though, from the scholarly black. Some have gone for a logical earthy green or brown, closer to nature and in line with Druid beliefs, but others prefer celestial white. The result is that they merge into the mist like heavenly creatures, floating in a disembodied state with nothing below the knee. Then there are those who, in party mood to welcome the solstice, have just let rip. One woman with a big, open face, a slash of red lipstick and long, white hair, sports a shimmering gold cloak. Another, close to her, shocking pink with gold leaves.

Her foliage is in the printed pattern of the material, but most of the assembled Druids have collected their own twigs and

Greeting the sun at dawn at Stonehenge.

flowers and pinned them to lapels, or wound them in their hair. Staffs are also much in evidence – some regular and straight, others twisted and obviously fashioned from branches. And under the cloaks, I notice, as my eyes and imagination adjust, are the sort of knee-length tunics worn by Robin Hood and his followers (or those imitating them in the TV versions), close-fitting, belted at the waist and good with tights.

I am starting to feel conspicuously under-dressed. The Barbour may be an essential element of the countryside code elsewhere, but not here. Fortunately, though, Druids are, as Theo has already pointed out, a tolerant lot. A middle-aged man in a white cloak over his black ecclesiastical cassock glides up to me, grinning. 'Matthew brings you a solstice gift,' he announces, using the third person and presenting me with an after-dinner mint in a bright blue wrapper.

I hover on the edge of various conversations, silently mar-velling at the resistance to cold of an elderly, slightly stooped man, his cheeks decorated with stripes of red, blue and white war-paint, who is sporting only a multi-coloured cotton sarong and open sandals. Alban Hefin or not, it is icy up on Salisbury Plain. Steve comes up and introduces himself. He is wearing a grey anorak and obviously feels a bond in our lack of finery. He is also a first-timer, he admits. He has been brought along by Druid friends whom he met while watching a solar eclipse in Spain in 2005. 'It is my hobby', he explains, 'to attend every eclipse, wherever it happens.'

Everyone is gathering good-humouredly by what, in five hours' time, will be the ticket office. The first to address us is one of two yellow-jacketed security guards, hired by English Heritage and discreetly policing proceedings without so much as a raised eyebrow. His message is brief. 'Can I just ask that you don't stand or sit or interfere with the stones?'

There is more enthusiasm for the next speaker, a middle-aged woman with a warm toothy smile and straight shoulder-length pale blond hair, pushed out to the sides by a red and gold striped scarf tied round her forehead like a bandanna. She introduces herself as Vix – short for Vixen, though she is more faithful family Retriever than cunning fox. She is, she announces, going to lead the ritual. This gets a small ironic cheer. Most forms of leadership are eschewed by Druids.

Are there, Vix asks, any volunteers to call on the gods of the four quarters? Hands go up almost at once. 'That's unusual,' she says. 'Normally, you need persuading.' Everyone laughs. As rituals go, this one is going to be *ad hoc*. 'And,' she continues, 'is there anyone wanting hand-fasting?' Two couples step forward. The older pair, who announce proudly they have come all the way from Germany, are among those who have already volunteered for the four quarters. Their enthusiasm now has an explanation. The other two, younger and more apprehensive, look round the group shyly and then back at each other. They have come all the way from Canada, the woman next to me confides. They were clearly expecting it to be warmer. The 'bride's' pretty purple dress leaves a lot of flesh unprotected.

Hand-fasting is the Druid equivalent of a marriage blessing.

So these two couples have travelled thousands of miles to plight their troth at dawn in front of a crowd of strangers. Such is the universal appeal of Stonehenge. Equating hand-fasting to marriage misses the point, though. For a start, Druid ceremonies have no legal significance. You have to go to a registry office beforehand. Or afterwards. 'The-piece-of-paper-marriage' is what Phil calls it. He and Theo have also done hand-fasting at Stonehenge. Today, in fact, is their anniversary. But it isn't a once-in-a-lifetime thing. It is staggered over three years – an incremental commitment, at intervals of a year and a day, that consists of a public binding together of the couple's hands in front of witnesses, which, when performed thrice, signifies a deeper, loving commitment. It is still not, however, quite a 'till death do us part' pledge. The hope is that love will endure, but failure brings no shame. 'I think that Druids are alone', Theo tells me, 'in having a ritual to mark the breaking up of a couple.' She clearly hasn't been to a liberal Anglican church for a while.

The procession is starting to move. I fall in as we go through the turnstile and into the subterranean passageway, decorated with murals of the stones. Above us the A360 trunk road that divides the car park from Stonehenge is silent. It is too early even for the lorries that plague this place by day on the busy roads that surround it and which have prompted talk of a road tunnel under the whole site. The participants are all talking, albeit quietly. There is a curious mixture of reverence and informality that is, I can't help thinking, very English. Anywhere else, if you gathered a group of people in outlandish costumes just before dawn and allowed them access to an ancient monument that is, for the rest of the time, shut off to the public, there would be a buzz, an irrepressible excitement, an underlying rush to get there, only partially held in check. But here, no one is rushing, or pushing, or shrieking. Take away the garb, and it feels rather like a group walking onto a village green, waiting to watch the cricketers emerge from the pavilion, in the sort of ritual so beloved of John Major – stoical, restrained and determinedly cheery as they clutch their glasses of warm beer. Appropriately so, for Druidry is, its adherents would argue, very much a native plant, as much a feature of the British landscape and character as old ladies on bicycles. And, despite those blood-curdling accusations that go with the name, no more threatening.

We emerge on the other side of the road. 'Can you feel the energy?' a portly man in Friar Tuck robes next to me asks. I smile, as polite a way as I can find of admitting I can't. Yet, as we head towards the stones, there is undoubtedly a kind of awe, of going where most visitors can't, of walking in well-trodden footsteps. And not just from three days ago, though the cigarette butts are all too visible.

The procession stops, a yard or so short of Stonehenge. Led by Vix, singly or in pairs, we begin to enter the circle through a slightly larger gap between two of the outer ring of standing stones on the north east of the circle. Some walk confidently through, as if entering the door of a familiar building, arms outstretched to greet the hosts on the other side. Others, though, pause, reverently, on the threshold to reflect. One man even performs a kind of jig.

Some – newcomers, I presume – are hesitant and unsure what to do. Perhaps it is the mystery of Stonehenge that is affecting them, the powerful effect of its wordlessness, its remarkable ability to have kept its secrets for so long in the face of every inducement to speak that humankind has been able to throw at it. Because, despite all the Druids' confident talk of it being a temple, no one has ever been able to prove, beyond reasonable doubt, precisely what this place was built for.

In spite of that – or even because of it – Stonehenge does undoubtedly have presence, and so, when it comes to my turn, I step forward tentatively and stop in the opening to see how it takes me. To my surprise I find my body, as if on autopilot, making to genuflect. It thinks I am going into a church.

I manage to curb the urge to dip my knee and, instead, simply stand still for a few moments surrounded on three sides by the mighty Sarsen stones to my left, to my right and above. Each is about 10 feet high, and so the effect is not unlike pausing in a door-jamb made for a giant. The lintel stone over the top is part of a now-broken chain that once must have linked all the original 30 vertical stones in this outer circle via mortice and tenon joints, taken straight from carpentry but here hewn into the grey sandstone.

I reach out my arms to touch the stones. They are strangely warm, despite the absence of anything but the promise of sun on the horizon. It puts me in mind of tree-hugging, often a source of derision, another of the Prince of Wales' odd habits, along with talking to his plants, but when tried – as I did a few years ago in a friend's wood with some ancient redwoods, already much older than any age I can aspire to – a surprisingly satisfying way of experiencing our own insignificance in the larger history of this planet.

And people have certainly been coming to Stonehenge from far and wide for a long time. In 2002, at Boscombe Down, two and a half miles to the south east, archaeologists found two bodies buried that date, they estimate, from between 2500 and 2300 BC. Chemical analysis of the tooth enamel of both men showed that one was from nearby Wessex, the other from the foothills of the Alps. Other excavations subsequently have unearthed the remains of immigrants from Brittany and Wales.

I move through into the sanctuary delineated by the outer stones and follow others in making a ritual circuit round the ambulatory formed between the tall, protective Sarsen stones, and on my inside the smaller, paler Bluestones that form a second barrier around the core of Stonehenge. Those that are still standing seem slight enough to invite not a simple touch, but a full-blown embrace. They are more the size and girth of an adult. However, as the thought passes through my mind, I catch sight on the horizon of a security guard, keeping his own vigil. I don't want to be ejected for breaking the few rules imposed on us.

In the centre, Vix is waiting, next to a fallen Bluestone that is serving as her altar. Her eager grin shows only the slightest hint of anxiety to get on, but betrays the fact that we are working to a timetable. Sun-up can't be far away. The final

Entering the circle of Stonehenge on Old Midsummer's Eve.

members of the procession are still entering the circle. They are illuminated from behind by a light that is turning a deep pink as the sun slowly climbs from its lair.

I find myself a spot in the ring of human bodies next to a plump, middle-aged couple. She has a garland of flowers tucked in her short, curly fair hair. He stands behind her, wrapping both of them in his voluminous brown cloak. Later, they tell me they are both nurses, and keep their attendance at such events to themselves. 'People might think we weren't to be trusted.'

We are closely packed and still as sunrise nears. For a monument made up of such massive slabs of stone, Stonehenge is surprisingly compact in the centre. Much smaller, indeed, than its extraordinary reputation.

*   *   *

Stonehenge, outwardly so strong a shape, feels from within like a ruin. But a ruin of what? That is the mystery that has drawn generation after generation of visitors, many of them intent on solving it. The few who have left convinced they have the key have, by and large, failed to convince others of their success in unlocking this enigma.

From inside the partially collapsed circle, the original layout of Stonehenge is not immediately apparent. There must once have been two complete rings, the outer one screening the inner in a fashion not seen in any of the other approximately 900 Neolithic stone circles around Britain. The large number of fallen stones, both Sarsens and Bluestones, is, however, sufficient to blur any overriding sense of form when you are standing in the centre. From some angles I glimpse it, and then I turn and the whole thing again feels utterly random. Which may have something to do with the fact that the arrangement of today is only 50-odd years old. In the 1960s, some stones that had collapsed of neglect were lifted and concreted back into what was assumed to have been their place.

In one sense, Stonehenge is a high-profile reproach to those who, since the eighteenth-century scientific enlightenment, have encouraged us to sweep 'primitive' religion to one side. In its place they have promised that scientifically based observations, calculations and investigations will provide the answer for everything under the sun, up to and including why the one that is rising on the horizon is about to be framed, perfectly, in one of the rectangular arches of Stonehenge. It cannot, in such a mind-set, be an accident that this place is perfectly aligned to the axis of the sun so as to provide a man-made device for capturing the dawn on the equinox. It must have been designed that way by 'primitive' religious folk. But when it comes to the why, the scientists come unstuck.

There has been no shortage of theories – that it was a healing shrine; an 'old Britain' war memorial; the place where ley-lines intersect; a primitive astrological observatory, to name but the most prominent. Yet to this day, no one can say with any sort of certainty who built it. Or even precisely why. Which, for me right now, and many of those who have come here in the past, is the key to its appeal. For the mystery allows it to be whatever we want it to be. Select an option from the list of possibilities provided by experts, or give free rein to our own imagination. Each age has projected its own preoccupations and ideas onto Stonehenge. So many ideas, so few facts. As a woman two along in the ring, with a large daisy on her forehead, later tells me: 'I'm very interested in science. I like reading it, but I never expect it to give me any answers. For them I come to places like this.' 'Don't you mean questions,' I query? 'No,' she is quite firm, 'answers.' They are not, I suspect, what scientists would call answers.

Officially this morning the stones are playing the part of an ancient Druid temple, a place where the assembled worshippers can honour their gods and link up with a faith that they believe has been suppressed and misrepresented down the ages.

*   *   *

There are, before you think I have a thing about scientists, a handful of secrets that they *have* managed to persuade Stonehenge to offer up. Such as the question of its age. It now seems to be a truth universally acknowledged that Stonehenge is around 5,000 years old, dating back to the Neolithic Age. Some parts may be older – evidence has been unearthed of wooden posts nearby from the Mesolithic Age, 7500 BC – while the most recent additions were made in 1600 BC. There is some dispute on the later time limit, with a team from Bournemouth University suggesting that they have found traces of medieval buildings at the site, but that view remains very much a lone voice.

The consensus, therefore, points to Stonehenge having gone through a cycle of development that has lasted for a total of around 6,000 years. That is in itself something to contemplate next to our own puny lifespans. Even the construction period of the inner core in which I am standing is thought to have extended over 1,400 years. The sheer timescale is one of the few things I have come across that merits the overused adjective 'awesome'.

There were, again in the broadest of terms, three distinct

phases to the construction. Some time around 3000 BC, the banked ditches or henges that surround the stone circle were constructed. (Stonehenge is not strictly a henge at all because it reverses the usual arrangement found in other henges of a raised bank with ditch inside.) Then, in stage two – around 2800 BC – a timber construction is thought to have stood in the centre of the henges. And then finally, in stage three – around 2400 BC – whatever timber construction was there was replaced by the stones. They went from wood to something more enduring at roughly the same time as the oldest of the pyramids was being built in Egypt.

The Sarsens are thought to have come from nearby Marlborough Downs, though the word 'nearby' has its limits when you think whoever brought them here didn't have anything we might call transport. But such logistical difficulties pale next to the journey apparently undertaken by the six-feet-tall Bluestones of the inner circle. Some still argue that these spotted dolomite rocks were swept here as part of a glacier, but most experts now agree that they were floated, dragged and hauled from Preseli Hills in Pembrokeshire, south west Wales, which is about 160 miles away as the crow flies. And that includes the small natural obstacle of the Bristol Channel/Severn Estuary.

So much for the facts; now for the speculation. Onto these bare bones, or bare stones, has been embroidered many an enticing tale. The first 'modern' theorist about Stonehenge was Geoffrey of Monmouth in the twelfth century in his rambling, gossipy and often fanciful *History of the Kings of Britain*. He posited that this was a burial place, or more precisely the burial place of the native British who were killed by invading Saxons in the fifth and sixth centuries. Not content with a plausible theory that the stone circle was a kind of monument to a native way of life that had been overwhelmed by foreign invaders, Geoffrey then also patched on an Arthurian legend. Stonehenge, he wrote, was either a replica, or indeed a transplanted original from Ireland, of a giant's ring. It had crossed the Irish Sea, he claimed, thanks to the skills of the magician

Merlin. Quite which skills, he doesn't specify, but presumably something akin to the transporter system on the Starship Enterprise in *Star Trek*. Furthermore, the Bluestones, Geoffrey of Monmouth suggested, had some sort of magical healing power, and Stonehenge would therefore have been a kind of pagan healing shrine.

The historical methods he used elsewhere in compiling his text would suggest that Geoffrey pieced this tale together from some existing folklorish stories, but neither his sources nor any earlier version of his tale have ever been found, save for the ancient local legend, in Wales, that attributes to the Preseli stones a magical healing power.

Where Geoffrey led, others followed. A revival of interest began in a monument that had, up to then, left precious little authentic trace in the history of the previous 3,000 years – i.e. since the final stages of construction in 1600 BC. Among the most significant of the new wave of speculators was Inigo Jones, often regarded as the first British architect, who, in 1655, published *Stong-heng Restored*, in which he described the stone circle as representing a Platonic ideal of architecture, modelled on ancient Rome. This claim – which he seems simply to have made up – prompted others to search for references to the place in accounts of the Roman occupation of England. They found nothing (though a recent dig has unearthed Roman coins at the site).

It was John Aubrey, in his 1665 *Monumenta Britannica*, who first raised the Druid connection. Rejecting the Roman link, he concluded, 'but all these monuments are of the same fashion and antique rudeness; wherefore I conclude that they were erected by the Britons and were Temples of the Druids'. He didn't offer anything more by way of explanation, but he had mentioned the words Druid and Stonehenge in the same breath. Which is why I am here today.

My fellow worshippers may be reluctant to endorse such an account, but it seems likely that their sort of Druidry can be traced back only to the seventeenth century. The name itself pre-dates this and was employed as a way of referring in general terms to the ancient Britons who had opposed the Roman invaders. There is a reference to 'Druids' fighting Roman troops on Anglesey, off the coast of north-west Wales, made by the Roman historian, Tacitus. In book fourteen of *Annals*, his history of the Roman conquest, Tacitus records:

> The druids were ranged in order, with hands uplifted, invoking the gods, and pouring forth horrible impreca-tions . . . The novelty of the fight struck the Romans with awe and terror. They stood in stupid amazement, as if their limbs were benumbed, riveted to one spot, a mark for the enemy. The exhortations of the general diffused new vigour through the ranks, and the men, by mutual reproaches, inflamed each other to deeds of valour. They felt the disgrace of yielding to a troop of women, and a band of fanatic priests; they advanced their standards, and rushed on to the attack with impetuous fury. The Britons perished in the flames, which they themselves had kindled. The island fell, and a garrison was established to retain it in subjection. The religious groves, dedicated to superstition and barbarous rites, were levelled to the ground. In those recesses, the natives [stained] their altars with the blood of their prisoners, and in the entrails of men explored the will of the gods.
>
> Tacitus, *Annals*, Book XIV, chapters 29–30

As for any more tangible connection between today's Druids and those imprecation-pouring fighters of Roman times, there is precisely none. The link was simply manufactured in the eighteenth century. It was the Anglican vicar, and biographer of Sir Isaac Newton, the Reverend William Stukeley, for example, who immortalized the notion of Stonehenge as a place of Druids. Stukeley was also an antiquary – a vocation that combined archaeology, oral history and a dash of magpie-like gathering up of assorted interesting bits and pieces. He argued in his 1740 book, *Stonehenge*, that the Druids were the precursors of Christians, and regarded with great reverence

Abraham, the Old Testament figure who today represents the strongest piece of common ground between the great mono-theistic faiths – Christianity, Islam and Judaism. Druidry, Stukeley wrote, apparently on the basis of little more than his own wish for it to be true, is 'so extremely like Christianity, that in effect, it differed from it only in this: they believed in a Messiah who was to come into the world, as we believe in him that is to come'. Stukeley even thoughtfully provided some hand-drawn illustrations to show how he imagined these Druids would have looked – ascetic sages in primitive hiking gear, sandals and hooded capes, carrying a wooden staff. The dress code is still in force today.

All this sensationalist musing by writers over an imagined pagan past for Stonehenge had, by the mid-eighteenth century, started to attract a substantial flow of visitors to the site. As their numbers grew, so did the theories about the exact nature of the Druid connection, each seemingly more lurid than the last. Those high-born Georgians who enjoyed the titillation of joining 'hell-fire clubs', such as that hosted by Sir Francis Dashwood at his seat, West Wycombe Park in Bucking-hamshire, descended on Stonehenge for outdoor dinner parties where they toasted the memory of their savage ancestors. In 1781, an Ancient Order of Druids was set up at a London pub by Henry Hurle, and within the decade it had established the practice of marking the equinox with a 'Gorsedd of Bards', albeit on Primrose Hill in London rather than at Stonehenge.

It took until 1905 for the modern Druids to come – or return as they would have it – to Stonehenge. Already, however, in the outwardly prim world of Victorian Christian England, the stone circle had gained an alluring reputation as a pagan place of darkness. Part of that was down to the Roman-tics. Both William Wordsworth and William Blake relished the idea of Stonehenge as a temple where cruel rituals and tortures had once been carried out. Turner painted Stonehenge melo-dramatically, illuminated by a violent thunderstorm which had claimed the life of the shepherd who lies in the foreground of his canvas, a dog howling at the side of the corpse. Meanwhile, the mystical Blake describes Stonehenge in 'Jerusalem' as:

> . . . a wondrous rocky World of cruel destiny,
> Rocks piled on rocks reaching the stars: stretching from
>   pole to pole.
> The Building is Natural Religion & its Altars Natural
>   Morality
> A building of eternal death: whose proportions are
>   eternal despair.

'Natural Religion' might serve rather neatly for the ritual that is going on today. The link between Stonehenge and nature and darkness made in Victorian times was never better realized than in the penultimate chapter of Thomas Hardy's 1891 novel, *Tess of the D'Urbervilles*. Tess and her husband, Angel Clare, are fleeing the law after she has murdered Alec Stoke-D'Urberville, the man who raped her and who has since blighted their marriage. They are walking on Salisbury Plain and approach Stonehenge by night, not realizing where they are.

'What monstrous place is this?' asks Angel. Tess, Hardy writes, hears the stones hum. 'The wind, playing upon the edifice, produced a booming tune, like the note of some gigantic one-stringed harp.' She falls asleep on the altar, sacrifice-like, the prelude to her arrest the next morning, her trial and her eventual execution. 'I like it very much here,' she murmurs. 'It is so solemn and lonely . . . with nothing but the sky above my face.' As she falls asleep, he sits thinking. 'In the far north-east sky, he could see between the pillars a level streak of light. The uniform concavity of black cloud was lifting bodily like the lid of a pot, letting in at the earth's edge the coming day, against which the towering monoliths and trilithons began to be blackly defined.'

*   *   *

The day is coming over the earth's edge in that same north-east spot at Stonehenge. As the orange upper lip of the sun swells steadily into what will soon be a lemon ball, a neat, rectangular shadow is creeping through the giant's door-jamb that has so recently welcomed us into the circle. This carpet of light is rolling like a hall-and-stairs runner across the rough grass towards the altar stone where Hardy imagined his Tess escaping, in nature's embrace and for one night only, the constraints of the world; and where today, Vix stands waiting to give the rising sun a suitable welcome.

Flanked by a row of assistants, her grin unwavering, she calls us to order. Her own route to Druidry, she later explains, was quite a pilgrimage, via Wicca, Christianity, Eastern religions, chaos and magic . . . and major surgery. 'I'd been searching but I still couldn't find anything that sat well with me and made me feel comfortable. Then I heard Bobcat' – the guru of this particular branch of Druidry – 'talking about the "spirits of the sacred grove". And it sang to me. So I explored it some more. The spirituality was as much about this land as about anything else, recognizing that this land is sacred, that these islands where my ancestors come from are sacred. Druidry hummed with that, compared to Christianity where that really strong Middle Eastern influence always felt to me edgy and sharp and spikey. It fits in this land. It's rooted in it. It fits me.'

Druids aren't great ones for committing things to paper. So Vix is not using any service sheet or prayer book. Spontaneity is prized above all, but if the words that emerge are poetic, so much the better. The order of bards within Druidry is prized for its creativity – in line with nature's own gifts – but it cannot be premeditated or, worse, preordained. Those are precisely the 'religion-of-the-book' constraints many here are seeking to escape.

Despite this non-literary, make-it-up-as-you-go-along bent in Druidry, a basic template of words and rituals does exist. The immediate source of much of this is one Iolo Morgannwg. Born in 1747 as Edward Williams, a name he later ditched in favour of his bardic-sounding Welsh moniker which translates as Ned of Glamorgan, Morgannwg claimed to have unearthed ancient Druid traditions and texts that had somehow survived in his native Wales throughout the periods of Roman and Christian persecution of home-grown beliefs. He made his 'finds' at precisely the right time to catch the rush of interest in a Druid past. However, the documentation he produced to back up his claims was dismissed by many at the time (and subsequently) as the work of a skilled forger. Morgannwg may have wanted to show that there was an authentic Druid set of rituals that pre-dated Christianity and which had been expro-priated by Celtic Christians. What seems much more likely, though, is that he based the rituals he 'rediscovered' on Celtic Christian texts, with the references to Jesus replaced by invo-cations to various nature gods.

So the basic structure of the ritual that Vix now embarks upon, even the words she uses, immediately resonates with my own Christian upbringing – and, presumably, with those of many of the individuals gathered here. It is at once reassuring and rebellious. So we start, for example, by honouring an alter-native Holy Trinity – the three elements of sea, sky and earth. Three of the team that has been flanking Vix step forward and, giggling, manoeuvre themselves into a triangle, standing back to back, hands joined behind them, and facing out onto the rest of us. 'Spirit of the sky, spirit of the sky, spirit of the sky,' they intone with melancholy longing that contradicts their broad smiles, 'I call to you – ye who hold this earth so softly, you give us the space and freedom in which to grow and develop. Spirit of the sky, spirit of the wind, spirit of the eye of the sun, spirit of the cloud and storm, spirit of the clear blue day, the black, star-studded night, I ask that you may bless our sacred space here this day. Know that you are honoured here, spirit of the sky. We bid you hail and welcome.'

They swing their arms as they speak, like children skipping along the pavement on the way to the school gates. It is an exuberant performance that sets a benchmark for all that follows. Vix now calls on those who have volunteered to take

The inner sanctum of Stonehenge is surprisingly cosy.

up their positions at the four points of the compass within the stones and offer a 'hail and welcome' to the gods of east, west, north and south. They do so with unabashed gusto, arms out-stretched, making up their prayers as they go.

It is almost 4.48 a.m. and time for the sun, finally, to join the party. The circle turns to face the north-east opening. We are silent as we watch. The argument that Stonehenge was designed for solstice celebrations rests on two facts – that the gap through which we entered and into which we are now gazing is larger than any other and lines up with the sunrise on the longest day. That much I can see.

The second piece of evidence is that the sunrise is also in line with the Heel Stone, a 16-feet tall boulder, well outside the main circle, but more or less dead centre through the enlarged opening in the Sarsen stones. It is believed to be the most ancient on the Stonehenge site.

A group of Victorian engineers, however, managed to disprove this claim of alignment in the 1860s, using the latest technology to show that the Heel Stone was slightly out. But then in the 1950s, when the old state-owned GPO was laying a cable close to Stonehenge – before it was properly protected – it was discovered that the Heel Stone was not a loner, but one of a pair, and that the solstice sunrise would, therefore, have been seen in perfect alignment between them.

As always with Stonehenge, the legend of the Heel Stone remains more powerful than such mundane details. The Heel Stone, Aubrey claimed, bore the mark of Merlin's foot as he ran from the devil. He evidently got this notion from a conversation with a local woman. Today, any such mark, if it ever existed, is invisible to this pair of eyes.

Having climbed so very slowly up from behind the eastern ridge, the sun suddenly puts on a burst of speed. Perhaps it senses us beckoning it to join us. Or it may be an optical illusion. Whatever, its bright shadow runs up Vix's body and onto her face as if seen on a speeded-up film. 'Blessed are you, lord of the sun,' she intones. As we all echo her words, the light leaps across onto the stones that surround her, revealing why they are called blue.

It switches on yet more energy among the participants. The circle breaks up as individuals and groups move into the centre to dance. Drums are picked up and beaten vigorously. One man plays his trumpet. Some of the women are clapping and ululating in what sounds like the whooping noises I associate with Roxy Music's 'Let's Stick Together'. From behind a stone, where he has evidently been changing, emerges a man dressed in a short green tunic and brown tights and sporting a mask and head-dress of stag horns. Jack-in-the-Green, a familiar figure at Morris Dancing displays is, in this Druid take, looking frisky and sinister. Like the Greek god Pan, Jack is lord of the wild places and fertility, a point Wilf, the man in the costume, makes plain as he waves the erect stick that he is carrying at groin level at each of us in turn.

It may just be natural inhibition, or too long spent in the stifling rigidity of mainstream Christian services, but this free-for-all suddenly feels very excluding. Partly because I can't vibrate my tongue, have always been a terrible dancer, and don't want to overexcite Jack. But also because the whole spectacle, while undoubtedly spontaneous, feels too much like every pagan cliché I've ever imagined, mixed together. To the lorry-drivers who are now passing by the perimeter fence, this display, glimpsed from afar, of a man in stag's horns waving a dildo in the middle of a group of apparently grateful women, will perpetuate all society's suspicions about what Druids really get up to. Closer up, however, it is about as threatening, uninhibited or spiritual as a rowdy hen party. As if to complete the stereotype, a crow flaps over us, making its own raucous cough noises.

What is it that has transformed a hitherto rather reverent and moving ritual? The sunrise, most obviously. Seasonal Affective Disorder (SAD) means that we are now well aware of the damage sun-deprivation can cause. But there is also the open invitation that Druidism, with its lack of definition, ideology, hierarchy, and even a well-documented past, offers to do-it-yourself religion. That is not to doubt the sincerity of those here, but rather to wonder if the hotchpotch of borrowed, and – in the sense of making demands on them – bowdlerized belief, has any point other than making them feel, as Vix would put it, 'comfortable' in their skins? They seem to be taking another famous line from Blake's 'Jerusalem' as their mantra, 'I must create a system, or be enslaved by another man's', without pausing long enough to consider the inherent danger he highlights in the line that comes next, 'I will not reason and compare: my business is to create'. What they present as so very old is, in fact, in the way they have tacked it all together, something new, created by them for them, and therefore somehow the very antithesis of the ancient site of Stonehenge where it is being acted out.

It is not, naturally, a view that Theo shares when I put it to her subsequently. 'What I don't like about other religions is precisely that – *their* transactional nature. That you make the right gesture and you get what you want, as in a transaction. Maturity says we have to move beyond that. It's not what I want, it's about my deepest relationship with the planet and the people around me.' She sees that I am not convinced and

Jack-in-the-Green frolics in the midsummer sun.

adds, by way of comforting me, 'but it can be hard to escape the patterns of the past'.

As we begin to pack up – vacant possession has to be handed over to the guards by 6.30 a.m. – two teenagers, dressed as sixties hippies and arms entwined, lead us out with a chorus of 'Lucy in the Sky with Diamonds'.

2

Bardsey Island

There is an island there is no going
to but in a small boat the way
the saints went, travelling the gallery
of the frightened faces of
the long-drowned, munching the gravel
of its beaches.

'Pilgrimages' from *Frequencies* (1978)
by R. S. Thomas (1913–2000)

The night before I take the boat to Bardsey Island, I lie awake in my hotel room in Criccieth, haunted by those frightened faces, and the imminent prospect of joining them in their watery grave. R. S. Thomas, Anglo-Welsh poet and Anglican churchman was, until 1978, vicar of Aberdaron, the fishing village at the tip of the Llŷn (pronounced 'Clean' 'but with plenty of spit', as one local advises me) Peninsula from whence set out the boats to Bardsey, also known in legend as 'the island of 20,000 saints'. The waters of Bardsey Sound, as Thomas knew, are notoriously treacherous.

Perhaps the Welsh name for the island – Ynys Enlli – captures it better. It translates as 'isle of the currents' or 'tide-race island'. Great surges of water funnel through the narrow strait that divides Bardsey from the mainland, making it an unpredictable and, on occasion, deadly place to venture out onto in a boat. Wrecks used to be big business on Bardsey. There were as many pirates there as saints, it is sometimes said. At the dawn of the nineteenth century, there was a resident population of 80, living off the land and sea. Today it is down to half a dozen.

Before turning in, I have called Tony the boatman, at his request. I wasn't panicking back then. Or not much. He doesn't confirm he's making the two-mile crossing until the night before – because of the currents. 'We're on,' he informs me with the blunt stoicism of one who tries to make a living out of this usually unco-operative sliver of sea.

Back in medieval times, in a coracle – stretched leather on a light wooden frame – with no map and only oars and a finger in the wind to judge the weather conditions (or so I imagine), the strait between the last flourish of the mountainous Welsh mainland and the island was considered so perilous that the Pope himself declared that three pilgrimages to Bardsey were the equivalent of one to Rome. Inaccessibility and holiness were officially equated here, as in heaven.

You won't find the papal formula recorded on parchment in the Vatican's archives, but the legend has survived because it rings true. Before the advent of trains, cars and planes, Rome would have represented a once-in-a-lifetime trek, risking life and limb on a journey that, for most pilgrims, would have had to be walked. Now, arguably, the equation has been reversed. From my home in London, I can get to Rome and back three times on a budget airline faster, cheaper and without nearly as much anxiety (save for my carbon footprint) as tomorrow's crossing is causing me.

I shift around in the bed, with its starched, sandpaper sheets, trying to stop thinking about drowning. As a child, this was the time when I would start the rosary, relying on its familiar pattern of prayers, repeated time and again, to lull me to sleep. Instead, I find myself distracted by how much the bedroom curtains are billowing in the breeze. It is a warm July night and I've opened the twin sashes for air, but now it looks like a gale is coming in. Is a storm brewing out in the Irish Sea? Might I have to wait on the shore in Aberdaron for days? Visitors to Bardsey often do. Or, worse, get stranded on the island. One regular has already told me that she had to wait for a safe passage home for three weeks, enough to try the patience of a saint, but mitigated by the hospitality of the permanent residents and their storerooms of baked beans. My stomach churns at the thought, but it is a better prospect than joining R. S. Thomas's gravel-munchers.

There is also, I reflect, the small matter of those 20,000 saints; all reputedly buried on Bardsey in the centuries after the warrior monk Cadfan founded a monastery there in 516. Having made the crossing once, they clearly decided not to risk it a second time. Which isn't how they would have seen it, of course. Their given reason had nothing to do with fear of drowning. Such was Bardsey's reputation back in the Middle Ages as an anteroom to heaven on the very edge of the known world, they simply couldn't bear to leave.

As the bright red display on the clock-alarm-teasmade ticks round to two a.m., a final, utterly irrational thought won't give way to sleep. A few days before, I interviewed for a newspaper Lorna Byrne, an Irish author whose autobiography, *Angels in My Hair*, was topping the bestsellers' chart in her homeland and had been bought by the American publishers of *The Da Vinci Code* for a six-figure sum. In it, Byrne recounts how she has always been able to see the guardian angels that hover in our shadows. The Celtic saints of Bardsey would, no doubt, have known exactly what Byrne meant, but I felt obliged to test her claim. What, I'd asked Byrne, does my guardian angel look like? She had dodged the question – 'I'm not allowed to say,' she had chided me – but added that, unusually, she could see my soul, albeit as if looking through a glass of water. At the time, I had been foolishly flattered. A prominent soul felt like an accomplishment. Now, however, I wonder if it was a premonition of my death by drowning.

Attempting the crossing is feeling ever more reckless. I've never been much of a swimmer since my mother, in her youth a champion in the pool, threw me in the local baths, aged eight, assuring me that we all naturally float. It was the last time I trusted her unthinkingly. I can still picture the beige tiles on the wall of the pool as I sank to the bottom.

I look over at my sleeping children – aged eight and eleven – one in the other twin bed and the other on a bizarre put-me-up

that folds up into an armchair, and wonder why on earth I have
dragged them along. To their doom. When I suggested the trip, it
sounded like a variation on the theme of a Famous Five adven-
ture. For Kirrin Island read Bardsey. I made it up to five by
including Margiad, a schoolteacher friend, who grew up locally
and still returns here regularly, plus her eight-year-old daughter.

My tendency has always been to take all reports of religious
visions lightly. 'Signs and wonders', the old Penny Catechism
labelled them, and told us to beware. Working at a Catholic
newspaper, as I did for eight years, you receive more than your
fill of reports of divinely inspired messages. We even had a
standard letter, ready to be sent out when a reader would
submit photographs of their newly stripped sitting-room floor
which, 'unmistakably', revealed the face of the Virgin Mary.
'Thank you for sending in your pictures which we return. It is
a special gift to be able to see such signs of God's presence in
our world. We, sadly, are not so blessed and cannot therefore
make out the image you refer to. With best wishes . . .'

God is not a conjuring artist, scattering clues for us to pick
up on living-room floors. And yet . . . once, at the *Herald*, the
young woman who claimed at the time to be experiencing
visions of the Virgin Mary every Sunday on Willesden Green in
north-west London, dropped in on us. Almost literally. She
had eschewed the usual entrance to the editorial office – via
the main staircase and the reception desk – and instead
suddenly appeared, shrouded in a large headscarf, at the fire
escape door, having climbed four stories up the outside metal
staircase. She refused tea and a chair. She 'just' wanted to tell
us that the Virgin had revealed to her that the world was going
to end that coming Sunday.

We were still making polite noises about this bombshell
when she departed as suddenly as she had arrived – so
suddenly we wondered if we had been the ones experiencing a
vision. As soon as she was judged out of earshot, we all
laughed. How these would-be mystics always over-reach themselves by making a claim that could easily be disproved! But on
that Sunday I was not the only one in the editorial team who

felt a little uneasy, and said an extra prayer or two, as we all
reluctantly admitted to each other when we regrouped on the
Monday morning.

However much an idea, or a suggestion, offends against
reason, logic or plain common sense, it can, if you have been
raised in a faith built on supernatural happenings and arbi-
trary punishments, easily get under your skin – especially
when in the shadow of somewhere with a mystical air such as
Bardsey. One of its admirers, the Anglican writer Donald
Allchin, once described it as 'a door through which we can
pass into another world'. Not a trap-door, note.

*   *   *

We arrive in good time for the boat at Porth Meudwy, a tiny
cove protected from the perils of the Bardsey Channel by twin
rocky promontories on either side. It is just to the north of
Aberdaron – or possibly to the west, the high-hedged, narrow,
winding country lanes having completely disorientated me, the
map-reading equivalent of a spin in a waltzer. Local lobster
fishermen now use Porth Meudwy's concrete slipway and
brutal stony beach as a safe harbour. Once, though, this was
known as the hermits' harbour and served as one of several
alternative embarkation points for medieval pilgrims heading
for Ynys Enlli. The water here is deeper closer to the shore
than at Aberdaron, Tony had explained.

We perch next to a tatty old shack on our waterproof picnic
rug and dig some snacks out of the rucksack for the children.
We've skipped breakfast, just in case, but the sea is now mercifully calm, the wind down to a whisper, and the sun high in the
sky. Someone, somewhere, is looking down benignly on us.

Signage for Porth Meudwy is minimal, and it has only been
thanks to the good offices of a local vicar, Evelyn Davies, that
we found it at all. She has accompanied us here but won't be
making the crossing this time, though she is a veteran. 'You'll
be fine,' she says with an air of authority as she departs. I let
myself be convinced.

Evelyn, a practical country woman in her late sixties, was one of R. S. Thomas's successors at Aberdaron, where she served for eight years until her recent retirement. In these straitened times for vocations, in the numerically small and disestablished Church in Wales, just as in its sister Church of England, she continues to minister to local parishes. But Evelyn also works tirelessly and with great passion to promote the ancient Celtic chapels and wells that once formed a pilgrim route up the spine of the Llŷn Peninsula, via places like Llang-wynnadl, Tudweiliog and Clynnog Fawr, and on to the cathedral city of Bangor, where a monastery was founded in 525 by Saint Deiniol (who was among the 20,000 to choose Bardsey as his final resting place).

In her years in Aberdaron, she has witnessed, Evelyn says, a marked but largely unreported and hence hidden spiritual revival, focused on Bardsey. 'The growing number of people I've seen come to make the crossing are sometimes straightforward tourists, but many are not,' she observes. 'Among these, many are not necessarily, or even often, Christian; but they do know something is missing that is not to be found in the materialism that the world offers as a cure-all. So they have started looking outside, have heard somewhere or read about Bardsey, and feel drawn to it. When they get there, they are amazed at its sense of peace.'

Some, once safely back on the mainland, come to Saint Hywyn's – Aberdaron's twelfth-century church, named after Cadfan's confessor, also buried on Bardsey. Evelyn estimates that it has around 10,000 visitors a year, some of them following the ancient pilgrim route down the Llŷn, but prevented by tides, currents, Tony's absence or time from undertaking the final lap to Bardsey. Many others, though, are back from the island and full of questions. They sit and reflect in the ancient church and, when she was around, talked to her. 'They were mostly un-churched, so I saw my role as simply to listen. They were often not used to talking about emotions and feelings, but Bardsey had unlocked something in them that needed to find a way out.'

Evelyn's does not count as a scientific study, but is instead an impression, gleaned on an unlikely front line. It has left her convinced that, as she puts it, 'something is being recreated in our midst'. One of her innovations when vicar was to invite visitors to write their name, or that of a loved one about whom they were concerned, on a pebble collected from the beach next to which the church stands. These would then be laid out in the south aisle, ever-present as prayers were offered during the year, until at the end of the tourist season, the schools' October half-term week, all the stones would be blessed in a special service and returned back to nature. R. S. Thomas, I can't help thinking, would have approved.

A white motor launch is heading towards the cove. A small group has gathered on the beach, including a ruddy-faced man with white hair, carrying a large cardboard box full of milk containers and loaves of bread. He is, it turns out, another local vicar, Nick Hawkins. He has come back to the mainland overnight – there is only one boat a day to and from Bardsey – to rustle up provisions for the two-week healing ministry that is taking place there at the moment. He also seems to have assembled a group of pilgrims with him. 'What's the crossing like?' I ask, my concerns still not entirely exorcized by the clement weather and Evelyn's optimism. 'The boat'll be like a mild fairground ride,' he tells me with such a radiant smile that it makes the prospect seem almost enticing.

Tony's boat, by now reassuringly substantial in size, has stopped about 20 yards away from the shore next to a small, grey inflatable dinghy tied to a buoy. That, it becomes apparent, is what is going to transport us out to the ferry in consignments of five or six. Safety fears to one side, it seems oddly fitting to leave the land in such a tiny flimsy craft, just as those earlier pilgrims would have done – even if after two minutes we are clambering clumsily out, and onto the much bigger boat.

Margiad finds herself seated next to an ancient, weather-beaten, waggle-toothed man in a tweed jacket who is carrying a shepherd's crook. They start talking in Welsh. Over three-

Pebble prayers on Bardsey.

quarters of those who live on the Llŷn speak Welsh. He breaks into English to demonstrate to the children – his swollen, black fingernails on display – how his crook isn't local. Its hook is good for catching fine-limbed, pampered sheep from 'the Downs in the south' by their back legs, he says, but on the Llŷn they need a bigger hook because the only way to stop Welsh mountain sheep in their tracks is to grab them round the neck and all but choke them into submission. I make a mental note to check the dimensions next time I see a bishop with his decorative staff of office.

The crossing takes no more than fifteen minutes. Once we've done with the *One Man and His Dog* lesson, and have then tried in vain to spot the seals and even dolphins said to inhabit these turbulent waters, Bardsey itself looms into view. My daughter thinks it looks like a sleeping cat, but the island that turns its humped back on the mainland reminds the others of a whale, basking on the surface of the Irish Sea. On a clear day, this distinct shape can be spotted, nuzzling the end of the Llŷn Peninsula, from all along Cardigan Bay.

The boat swings down past the great dome of steeply falling cliffs and towards the tail of the cat/whale, puny and shrunken in comparison to its upper quarters. It is flatter and has a red and white painted, square-towered lighthouse standing at its tip.

I look back to where we have come from as we prepare to land. The clear skies make for panoramic views. Behind are the hills of the Llŷn that climb towards the peaks of Snowdonia. To the south, Cardigan Bay forms a smooth but increasingly indistinct arc. And away to the north, on the horizon, lies the shadow of Anglesey.

If Bardsey's Welsh name is all too readily understandable, the origins of the English alternative are more obscure. Precise scholars suggest that it is Scandinavian and perhaps a reference to a one-time Viking resident of the island called Bard or Berd. The more romantic prefer the notion, enticing but impossible to prove, that once Bardsey was home to a Druid colony of poets – or bards. The presence of Anglesey, Ynys Môn, gives some sustenance to the notion. For, as I discovered at Stonehenge, a prime authenticated record of Druids in ancient Britain was in Tacitus's account of the Roman assault in AD 60 on Anglesey.

The boat pulls into a makeshift harbour. The breakwater consists of metal cages of rocks, strapped together and stacked up against the tides. They also form the rough causeway we walk along between disembarking and setting foot on Bardsey proper. Only the shepherd stays on board. 'I've seen enough,' he tells us. Tony looks unperturbed. 'Be back by three,' he announces as he waves us off.

Bardsey divides neatly into two. The hump of Mynydd Enlli rises on the mainland side of the island. It isn't quite a mynydd – or mountain – and, at 547 feet, certainly won't meet the qualifying standard of 2,000 feet demanded by the Ordnance Survey. You can see, however, why it got the name, because it is still big enough to block out any hint that Bardsey is part of anything that lies to the east. Sheltering behind Mynydd Enlli, the rest of the island is low-lying, and out of sight and earshot of the modern world. Even the 'essentials' of a mobile phone and Radio 4 FM signal are obliterated, leaving those in its wake to concentrate instead on the view westwards of patterns of uninterrupted sky and sea.

This lee-side of Bardsey is cultivated. In the 1770s, the island's resident farmers used to supply oysters, seed corn and butter by boat to Liverpool. There were enough of them 50 years later so that when Lady Maria Stella, the young second wife of the island's then owner, Baron Newborough, came over in the summer, she could anoint a king from among the community with a crude tin crown made by the lighthouse keeper (and now kept in Liverpool's Maritime Museum). There was even a school, which in a 1934 photograph boasted eleven pupils, all of them taught in one room by the sister of the resident Presbyterian minister.

If the early saints came to look into the world beyond what they believed lay off Bardsey's west shore, it was the lure of modernity to the east that eventually proved too great for the working people of Bardsey. As with other isolated offshore communities in the second half of the twentieth century, it saw its young depart for the mainland and take the future with them. By 1964 the population had dwindled to almost nothing when the celebrated travel writer, Eric Newby, described Bardsey as a 'disenchanted isle' that faced complete abandonment.

The fields today, though, are well kept, the whole place now run by a trust which merged the farms into a single entity and generates income by renting out various of the farmhouses to summer visitors. These holiday lets stand in a rough line up the centre of the island – hump to one side, fields to the other. It is towards them – civilization, Bardsey style – that we are drawn.

We walk along the rough-hewn pathway that counts as Bardsey's main road with Nick Hawkins, plus his loaves of bread and pilgrims. One couple, retired hoteliers from nearby Abersoch, have been looking out across the water to Bardsey for 30 years. What persuaded them finally to come? 'Time on our hands, curiosity, I don't know,' says the husband. 'And over the years we have heard so much about how special it is here. Special in the sense of different. We thought we ought to find out for ourselves.'

They branch off and we are left behind, all alone, the children running ahead to climb the high grass banks that enclose the pathway. Margiad and I walk slowly, taking in the raw beauty of the place, saying nothing. It takes a few minutes for it to sink in. The wind has dropped to nothing and, with it gone, there is no man-made noise on Bardsey. The island has managed to absorb the small group that came ashore with us into its silence. Save for the odd bird chirping (Bardsey is big with bird-watchers, drawn to see the Manx shearwaters that come here from the South Atlantic to breed), there is only grass, sea, sky and . . . nothing. The devil, C. S. Lewis wrote in his *Screwtape Letters*, 'detests' music and silence. What more perfect place then for a community of monks?

Lives today are so very noisy – 24-hour news bulletins, 24/7 shopping malls, Blackberries, mobiles, sirens, the neighbours rowing through the walls. Silence has been almost completely lost as a virtue. Once we marked death with the silence of a period of grieving. Now we rush noisily about trying to 'get over it'. Even in libraries and churches, traditionally deep pools of silence in the midst of the cacophony of the world, there is usually a constant low murmur. Here on Bardsey, though, is a pure form of the silence that must have drawn those medieval pilgrims in the first place. Along with its close relative, solitude.

*   *   *

Solitude, though, sits uncomfortably with the idea of 20,000 saints buried on so small an island as Bardsey. That's roughly 44 for each of its 450 acres. Perhaps, though, the figure should not be taken literally. Some feel it is simply a marketing catch-phrase – a convenient myth to peddle to get people's pulses racing and keep the tourists making the crossing in the summer months. They are right in one way. Celtic myths and legends have a tendency towards inflation, exacerbated of late by them being so in vogue with those looking for an alternative to 'official' Christian doctrine and practice. Witness the success of former Catholic priest John O'Donohue's 1997 word-of-mouth best-seller, *Anam Cara*, a book of Celtic spiritual wisdom.

What certainly does appear to be true is that from the sixth century onwards, Christians from the north and west coasts of Wales, as well as pilgrims from further afield, made their way to Bardsey, where many then stayed to see out their days. The Celtic variety of Christianity, lived out in the fifth century by monks in Ireland, who then carried it with them on their missionary journeys across the Irish Sea (sometimes called the 'Celtic Mediterranean'), forms the backdrop to the founding of the monastery on Bardsey by Cadfan in 516. A Breton nobleman, he travelled, along with a group of pious highborn friends, all immersed in the Celtic tradition, to the west coast of Wales and founded monasteries, culminating in setting up an abbey on Bardsey dedicated to the Blessed Virgin Mary.

Establishing a community on Bardsey would, in theory, have ruined the wonderful silence of the place, if only by importing too many people to leave the island genuinely peaceful; but the monks of Celtic Christianity followed the example of the Desert Fathers, hermits and ascetics such as Saint Antony (c. 251–356), who dedicated their lives to prayer and hard manual labour in loosely knit communities in the wilderness of the Egyptian desert. The Celtic monastic communities similarly sought out-of-the-way, wild places – islands were a particular favourite – where they would not be distracted from hearing the word of God. These informal groupings would live as solitaries, but side-by-side.

There was both an intensity and a separateness in the enclosure of the island. Each monk would have his own hermit cell or hut, but these would have been gathered round a central well. There would have been occasional community meetings, but the core isolation of the Desert Fathers had, on its translation to Europe via such figures as Saint John Cassian in the early fifth century, taken on an added dimension. There was,

in the vocation of these Celtic monks, an element of evangelization. They combined lives of prayer and solitude with the
call to go out and convert local people to Christianity – usually
by force of example.

Over the centuries, however, that Celtic way of being
Christian was modified by contact with the more collective,
ordered, Roman approach to ritual and belief. Rome organized the Church into dioceses, with a bishop at the top,
answerable ultimately to the Pope. The Celtic way was for
abbots to exert a looser and more personal jurisdiction over
surrounding areas. Bardsey was far enough from Rome, and
famous enough as a place of pilgrimage, to maintain its independence.

In the *Book of Llandaff*, compiled in the middle of the
twelfth century, Bardsey is praised 'for its sanctity and dignity,
because there were buried therein the bodies of 20,000 holy
confessors and martyrs'. It seems to have managed to maintain
its asceticism at a time when other ancient monastic estab-
lishments were succumbing to corruption of ideals. The late-
twelfth-century traveller and chronicler, Giraldus Cambrensis,
describes Bardsey as 'inhabited by very religious monks'. He
adds, in a line still often quoted, that the island 'has this wonderful peculiarity that the oldest people die first, because
diseases are uncommon, and scarcely any die except from
extreme old age'.

So it was holy *and* healthy, both on account of standing
apart from the world. And, it should be added, blessed.
Legend has it that it was an angel who promised Saint
Lleuddad, Cadfan's successor as abbot, when on his death bed,
that henceforth no one on the island would die while there was
someone older living there.

Bardsey is awash with legends, an indication of its importance as a place of pilgrimage in the Middle Ages. You don't
fashion miraculous stories about a place no one has heard of
or visited. One has it that Saint Llawddog, a sixth-century
descendant of royal blood from the north of Britain, once
milked a cow over a well on Bardsey, and afterwards the well

produced milk instead of water to nourish visitors. Another suggests that Bardsey is the final resting place of that central figure in Arthurian legend, and Britain's sacred landscape, Merlin the magician.

Some time after Giraldus's visit, however, the abbey finally lost some of its traditional independence when it became a branch of the Augustinian order. At various stages thereafter it is recorded that it held land on the mainland and received tithes from Aberdaron. It must eventually have gone into decline for, by 1537, when it was dissolved, along with all monasteries on the orders of Henry VIII after his break with Rome, the abbey contributed the meagre sum of £46 to the King's commissioners.

Our slow ramble up from the harbour has now reached the line of buildings that underscore the slope of Mynydd Enlli. The children are fascinated by the tiny schoolhouse, its windows painted a jolly bottle green and now used as a cottage by holiday-makers. 'Where is the playground?' my daughter wonders aloud. Why would they need one, I point out, when the whole island is like one big playground. City child that she is, taught from an early age to regard strangers with suspicion and to keep within fixed boundaries that delineate what is safe, she looks unconvinced. For her, as it was for medieval pilgrims, Bardsey is another world.

Further up the path is an old stable, housing Bardsey's very own public toilet – operated on 'compost' principles and featuring, next to a supply of what smells like freshly mown grass clippings, a notice that reads 'Please cover with grass-cuttings when you have finished'. And beyond it lies all that is left of Cadfan's abbey. The ruined thirteenth-century tower, its grey, flinty stones too crumbly to risk being climbed, exudes only a sadness, as all abandoned buildings do, and affords little by way of clues as to how this remotest of monastic communities might once have operated. Whatever essence remains, it is not in the buildings.

What about 20,000 graves? Do they offer a connection with the past? Well, there is a walled graveyard, next to the tower, and even a memorial stone imploring 'Respect the souls of the 20,000 saints whose remains lie close to here'. 'How close?', asks my son, nervously hopping around in the overgrown grass of the cemetery, as if fearful of stepping on dead bodies. I can't decide whether to tell him about the local legend that says the ghosts of some of the 20,000 have been seen wandering Bardsey's shoreline late at night, perhaps waiting for the elusive return boat to Aberdaron. Will it frighten him? Especially if we get stranded here overnight. But isn't it also the point of Bardsey? Namely, that the memory of those saints isn't in the ground, or indeed cloaked in ghostly silhouettes, but somehow in the air, to be breathed in?

I try to mention the 'mass graves' as quickly and undramatically as I can. Excavations have found evidence of bodies buried together in the twelfth century on Bardsey. He appears to hear since he stops hopping, but asks no more.

There are many theories about the origin of the claim to be the final resting place of 20,000 saints. One suggestion is that some at least were the survivors of a royal massacre in 613 of the monks of Bangor-on-Dee, North Wales, another monastery founded by Deiniol. They fled to Bardsey in the hope that the treacherous currents of the Sound would protect them from their pursuers. On the run, the escaped monks ended up living and dying here, in a kind of glorious haven for outlaws.

Another theory holds that many of the 20,000 did not come here as pilgrims in their lifetime and then stay on to die, but rather arrived after death to be buried in what was regarded as the ultimate holy soil. In the twelfth century, when the tides permitted in the summer months, boats would pass along Cardigan Bay, collecting the corpses of wealthy, recently dead Christians from tiny stone churches on or next to the beaches, and then transport them to Bardsey to be buried. To secure such a grave, they would have had to bequeath part of their wealth to the abbey on Bardsey.

Such individuals were not then saints in the modern sense, but Celtic Christians had a different notion of what it was to

The ruins of Cadfan's abbey.

be a saint from that promoted today, principally by Catholicism which has made canonization into an industry. Its production line demands exceptional (and sometimes controversial) individuals, chosen by Church commissions on account of their supposed virtues in life and the miracles that have been achieved through their intercession from beyond the grave. By contrast, being labelled a saint in Celtic circles often indicated simply that the person was a Christian leader, a missionary, a hermit or even just a good person. In such a context, the claim that 20,000 devout souls may have been buried on Bardsey over the 600 years after Cadfan's foundation, is suddenly not so implausible. If anything, it makes the whole place more accessible – not the graveyard of the pious heroes of the Church, a cut above the rest of humanity even in death, but the final home of those, like all of us, who try to lead decent lives.

The sun is high in the sky and stomachs are rumbling after that missed breakfast. The shadow of the monastery's ruined tower seems like a good place for a picnic. I resist the temptation to keep something back from our provisions in case we get stranded. It isn't even that tempting. My irrational fears are beginning to be warmed away. Or is the island beginning to work its magic on me? Speaking through the silence, albeit in Welsh which I won't understand? Would I welcome the chance to be forced to listen over a longer timescale?

Before I can come up with an answer, an old woman emerges from one of the nearby barns. A small sign by her gate announces that there is an exhibition inside. She is Bardsey's artist-in-residence. In her paint-splattered smock, with her dark, greying hair pinned up at the back of her head, she fits a stereotype. We start talking. This is, she says, her third summer on Bardsey, but she goes back to the mainland for the winter. It isn't, she reflects, somewhere for the faint-hearted, with no mains electricity. Where does she paint? 'Oh, mostly in a stable. All the best people are in a stable.' A throw-away line as she wanders off down the track, but the religious references never seem far away on this island. Perhaps that is what the 20,000 came for. They wanted to live and die in an un-ashamedly holy atmosphere. 'But surely,' Margiad reflects, while handing over another sandwich, 'they could have got that elsewhere. On the Llŷn' – she says it properly – 'there would have been plenty of holy places and it was even more remote then than it is now.'

What, though, did Bardsey offer that was extra? However remote a part of the mainland may be, islands have that extra physical degree of separation and, in the case of the monks of Bardsey, potentially a certain added independence of church authorities that sprang from being so hard to reach. You can imagine the bishop's enforcer arriving to lay down the law about forms of prayer, fasting, or whatever, and then being stranded here for weeks before finally going native and falling in with the Bardsey way of doing things.

Moreover, the experience of exile from your regular com-munity – if only across the narrow but dangerous strait that separates Bardsey from Aberdaron – can, if children's litera-ture is to be believed, allow individuals to flourish and even acquire hitherto unsuspected powers. Think Mowgli in Rudyard Kipling's *Jungle Book*.

Or is it the complete absence on Bardsey of any distraction from God? It is certainly an extreme sort of place. And that journey from the mainland, risking a kind of martyrdom in the Sound in order to cut yourself off physically from the rest of civilization, suggests a kind of extremism. In an age before accurate maps, Bardsey would have felt like the end of the known world, the brink, the edge of the abyss. To come required an act of faith. To stay, even more.

Bardsey may be an odd place in which to think about Tibetan Buddhism, but it keeps coming into my mind. It's the remains of those 20,000 saints who lie under our picnic rug. Tibetan Buddhism, more so than its close relatives in Eastern religions, has a strong sense of the presence of death in the midst of life. The Indian master, Padmasambhava, 'the Lotus-born', is credited as the founder of Tibetan Buddhism (though, like the 20,000 saints, some doubt he ever existed). He is said to have abandoned palaces to live on the charnel ground, a cemetery where dead bodies were traditionally left to rot as a reminder to the faithful of the unimportance of the human body within the cycle of *samsara* – death and rebirth, repeated many times over in pursuit of the highest state of karma. (There was also the small practical question of the lack of fuel to burn corpses, but no matter.) Padmasambhava found the charnel ground an excellent place for meditating on the importance of letting go of your ego and your attachment to this life. It provided, he believed, the impetus to see beyond life and death to ultimate enlightenment.

Bardsey, I can't help thinking, with so many corpses on so few acres, was and remains a kind of charnel ground. Was that – is that – part of its pull? Not that there is rotting flesh, of course, but it is palpably somewhere where the division between the living and the dead is blurred.

In the Tibetan *Book of the Dead*, much is written of *bardo*, a transitional state that covers both the approach of physical death and the early stages on the journey to eternal enlightenment, which can happen only when you are dead. The two are seen as one. Having witnessed the deaths of my parents, and a handful of others for whom I felt a great affection, I believe there is a profound wisdom in the notion of *bardo* that is utterly over-looked by the Western religious tradition. I have watched these people, before they die, enter into a state that is somewhere between life and after-life. They are half here, half somewhere else. Their thoughts are drawn away from the everyday and carry us with them towards the ineffable. And when they have died, they remain very vivid for a short period, so much so that conversations, imagined of course, can still be had with them, or their presence felt in rooms or favourite locations.

Bardo too may have been understood – albeit by another name – by those elderly saints who came here to Bardsey, away from the world and its cares and concerns, to prepare for and contemplate death and then move to the 'other side'. As the oldest prepared for death, the others waited their turn, already with one foot in the next world, geographically, emotionally and spiritually. Was that the uniqueness of Bardsey?

*   *   *

A modern seeker amid the silence and solitude of Bardsey was the Anglican nun, Sister Mary Helen. She lived here as a hermit for 25 years until her death in the 1990s, in her mid-eighties. Her hermitage remains as she left it, in the enclosed farmyard next to Carreg Fawr, once the sturdy home of the Newboroughs when they were in residence on their island. Her oratory in particular is kept as a kind of shrine, a reminder of the hermit tradition to which Bardsey has long played host. A small icon of the Madonna and Child is on a prayer stand by the entrance, timeless and otherworldly, eschewing, as the Orthodox tradition demands, the human side that is part of Western religious art, in favour of something more transcendent. There is a small crucifix lying on another table, while the walls are roughly plastered and whitewashed. There is a text, highlighted on a piece of card: 'The angel surprises us, the heavens open. Our little island is the world's centre. Welcome to joy.' The text is by a modern writer of prayers, Jim Cotter, but, in this context, manages to belong to Bardsey.

We've come to the oratory to attend one of the healing services run each summer for two weeks by the Order of Jacob's Well, a group of lay and ordained Christians. Nick Hawkins is part of the order, and the loaves he brought over on the boat were supplies for those based for the fortnight in Carreg Fawr. The farmyard outside the oratory has been laid out for a service. At the entrance, an elderly woman in a T-shirt that announces she is 'Ageing to Perfection' welcomes us in. They have borrowed Evelyn Davies's idea with the stones. We are all given one and a marker pen and invited to write on it the name of someone we feel is in need of prayers.

While the children embrace this craft activity, I seek out the Revd Mike Endicott who is leading the Jacob's Well healing mission on Bardsey. He is standing outside the front door to Carreg Fawr, a tall, imposing man with steely-grey hair and a thick beard. He is also blind, but brushes it aside as a minor inconvenience. Indeed, his whole manner is matter-of-fact, almost jokey, and decidedly non-PC. There's something of the self-made businessman to him; affable, keen to cut through the bullshit, but absolutely sure that he's right. What's Jacob's Well all about, I ask? 'To find people who are interested in applying the gospel to sick folks,' he replies, 'and encourage them, teach them, raise them up, pray for them.'

The order has something like 150 licensed ministers in the UK and is expanding into South Africa. It is ecumenical, and not all licensed ministers are ordained. 'But you are all Christians?' 'Oh, absolutely,' replies Mike, with none of that slight embarrassment you find about the C-word elsewhere in multi-cultural Britain. 'We follow the healing ministry of Christ.' He got involved 20 years ago – 'when I first became a Christian.' Someone took him to a healing service. 'I was amazed because they were actually singing about Jesus rather than Victorian poetry. Do you know what I mean?' The rhetorical question is a favourite device. He hardly leaves a pause before continuing.

'They were teaching about Jesus rather than telling me how to behave. I remember getting up to go and the person who took me said, "Wait and see this", and people starting praying with each other. I thought, "Wow". I got hooked there and then.'

He is an ordained Anglican minister – by Rowan Williams, the Archbishop of Canterbury who, in a previous life, was head of the Church in Wales and is also a patron of the order – and based in Cwmbran in the valleys of South Wales. He travels the country and the globe with his healing ministry, but has been coming to Bardsey for the past four years. 'I have a vested interest in this island,' he confides, 'because if you go back into the 1500s and look at the Welsh historians, they are writing about this place and saying it's extraordinary because no one's ever ill here, and it's the old people who die first. Not a natural thing to say now, but they claimed then it was because of the efficacious glare of the saints. They believed in those days that where you were buried was your place of res-urrection. So they came here to die.'

His church history may be slightly seat-of-the-pants stuff, but he says it with great conviction. And does he believe that something of that past remains alive on Bardsey today? Of those resurrected saints? 'Struggle how you like, you couldn't fill this island with tourists, so you are very much left alone with God and the elements. A sense of that past? Oh gosh, yes, you do. We are here to melt our spirituality back in with the historical spirituality of the island.' And to heal? 'Yes, every-thing, the whole lot. I've experienced miracles, thousands of them, too many to remember, all through prayer. Tons of it. It is easier to heal in some countries than others. It is harder in Britain exactly because we are more sceptical.' Bardsey, then, is a rare place, outside mainstream British secular culture, where visitors can be persuaded to set that scepticism aside.

It is often said that when you lose one of your five senses, the others are strengthened by way of compensation. I had a dear and very religious friend who, after losing her sight halfway through life, believed she had a heightened awareness of what one might call spiritual vibes – presences in old houses, holiness in places she'd visit. Does Mike, I find myself asking, have, as a result of his own loss of sight, additional antennae that pick up some of that history of belief in the air of Bardsey? He laughs heartily. 'I don't think so. It is a perception that people have but it is not true.' It clearly isn't the moment to broach with a minister who claims to have been part of thousands of healings the question of whether he prays that his own loss of sight be cured.

The residents of Carreg Fawr are beginning to walk past us and over to the farmyard chapel. It is time for Mike to join them. He takes me by the shoulders and lines me up alongside him. Gripping my arm firmly, he tells me to lead him across. Inside, some 20 people are gathered. A few I recognize from the boat-trip, others from the doorway of Carreg Fawr. The children and Margiad are waiting for me on one of a collection of church pews facing forward. At the front, sheltered from the sun by the branches of a rough gorse tree, is a circle of green plastic garden chairs, the sort you get from your local DIY shop. In the centre of the ring is an enormous pile of pebbles.

One of Mike's colleagues starts off with prayers. The simple liturgy draws on Celtic texts. One line, about discovering 'sound from silence', strikes a particular chord. You have first to be still and silent so that you can hear other sounds. Mike then gives a robust sermon. From a distance, there is something Charlton-Heston-as-Moses about him in this wilderness setting. 'I'm going to talk about Christ's healing ministry,' he begins, standing in the circle. 'I don't want us to think it's just about in-growing toenails. I mean it is, but there is a lot more.' His delivery is messianic, his words sincere but familiar – that we need to pay more attention to Christ. 'The true light of the world which is Jesus has gone round the back a bit recently. Right? Yeah. Do you understand where I am coming from? He's coming back but right now he's disappeared off the face of the earth. Except his spirit.'

Mike is not, he tells the congregation, a man to dwell on the negative. 'I don't like this idea of looking at yourself all day long thinking how miserable you are, but I do think it is real of us to recognize that if only we could polish up the surface a bit, buff it up, we would be better reflectors of his light into the world. So I'd love you to come into the circle, and if you can think of anything specific, that's great, but if you can't think of anything specific and just want a polish so you can be a better reflector of Jesus's life and grace in the world, that would be good too.'

It sounds pretty open-ended and uncommitted, enough to persuade me to abandon simply looking on and try out participating. Buffing-up sounds uncontroversial. Pleasant even. And Mike's handmaidens are encouraging people forward. There is a steady stream of others taking seats in the circle. I'm lucky to get one.

As I sit waiting my turn, three members of Jacob's Well are standing around the man opposite, their hands held aloft over his head. 'Holy Spirit of the Loving God, flow into this beloved child, healing where there has been harm, strengthening where there is weakness, and lifting the heart to reflect his glory.'

Finally they come to me. They begin by wrapping my head in a beige pashmina, an odd sort of gesture on such a warm day, and one whose symbolism is neither obvious nor explained. Then I am anointed on my forehead with a sweet-smelling oil. The group gathers round and repeats the prayer. When they finish, they stand back, hands still held aloft, as they subside into silence.

I'm not sure what I think might happen, but I am aware of checking every inch of my body and mind for signs of change. Not, if I'm honest, with much expectation of finding anything, but not entirely ruling out the possibility either, and therefore worrying about having my whole life turned upside-down. I suspect that Mike and his ministers would say that I am insufficiently open to the possibility of healing, polishing, buffing-up, whatever it is called. And hence I feel no different.

I try, as I had the night before, to empty my mind of thoughts. It has always been the barrier I encounter to praying. As an aid, I fix my eyes on the pile of stones at my feet in the

centre of the circle and make a rough estimate of how many
there are – perhaps as many as 200, a sign of how many people
have already passed through this outdoor church in the past
fortnight. I begin to read the names inscribed on each.
Instantly I recognize my daughter's handwriting. She has
already whispered to me, back in the pews, that she wrote her
grandfather's name, Alan, on her stone. Only the rough
surface seems to have made her letters go haywire. It reads
Alien. I suppress an urge to laugh.

The ministers take my smile as a sign that I am ready to
return to my seat. They remove the pashmina. Still the farmyard is silent. As I step away from the circle, my daughter turns
to Margiad and says in a whisper that in Bardsey's overween-
ing silence comes out too loud and carries to the whole assembled group, 'Didn't Daddy look silly in that scarf?' After
which, it is hard to rekindle any sort of atmosphere of prayer
and reflection.

The service is at an end. The 'Ageing to Perfection' usherette
is waiting at the doorway to collect our service sheets. 'Do you
feel polished?' she asks chirpily. 'I saw you smiling.' I immediately start apologizing and recounting the tale of Alan the
Alien. 'Don't worry,' she says, beatifically to my daughter,
'God knows who you mean.' I envy her easy confidence.

As we hover in the gateway, I find myself standing next to
another youngish woman who went into the circle to be
prayed over. We both, it seems, want to know what effect it
had on the other. I own up first. It was unusual, I say, outside
my daily experience and therefore welcome, and not in any
way negative, but neither was it momentous. 'You just had the
polish, then,' she says. Her grin suggests she had something
more.

We walk away from Carreg Fawr without saying very
much. The children run on ahead, across the meadow that separates it from Bardsey's one and only pedestrian thoroughfare.
'Weren't you tempted?' I ask Margiad. 'For a moment,' she
replies. Her own upbringing was Anglican, and she remains,
she says, very open to religious experience. 'But there was

something about it that reminded me of a Derren Brown show.' The TV illusionist often calls people up on stage as guinea pigs. 'I couldn't quite take it seriously.'

*   *   *

Donald Allchin, the Anglican writer who is a contemporary chronicler of Bardsey, has referred to the island in one of the books I read before coming over as a 'thin place', not in the sense that it is small and insignificant, though of course geographically it is, but rather that it is a place where the barrier between this world and the world of the spirit dissolves.

As we head back towards the harbour, where the boat is waiting, I mull over his phrase and know what he is getting at. There is something literally outside the ordinary about Bardsey because of its geography and unique history, but there is also something enigmatic about the place too. Or, more precisely, too subtle to be captured in a single visit or pilgrimage. That may be the real reason the 20,000 saints didn't come back to the mainland. Not a mundane fear of drowning in the perilous Sound, but a need to probe further, to get under the skin of the island, a task that could only be achieved by seeing out their days there.

Certainly it offers no instant get-away-from-it-all booster. Or certainly, even on as benign and blessed a day as today, no satisfactory one. The healing service was, for me, too crude in its attempt to harness the past to the present, but behind the silence of Bardsey that past does somehow whisper to you. Only in a language I cannot understand. Yet.

'Respect the souls of the 20,000 saints whose remains
lie close to here.'

3

The Wells of Derbyshire

Oh, come to the water all you who are thirsty.

Isaiah 55.1

My mother was outraged, I recall from childhood, when household water started to be charged for separately in the 1970s. 'It used to be included in your rates,' she pointed out irately in letters of complaint to the local town hall which she wrote but made my father sign. 'Now you've separated it out, you will soon be charging as much for it as the rest of the rates put together.'

Not far wrong as economic predictions go, but her obsession with maintaining a tight domestic economy – our central heating system seized up through lack of use and outgoing phone calls were banned until after six p.m. when the cheap rate applied – disguised a more basic and generally held assumption, namely that water comes down from the skies plentifully as rain and should therefore be free. So no expensive cordials or juices for us when we were thirsty. 'There's plenty of water in the tap,' we were told. As far as she was concerned, we might just as well stand in the back garden with our heads tipped back and mouths open, so as to drink in the raindrops direct and cut out the middle man.

And they certainly did come down in abundance in Macclesfield, the Cheshire town where I spent the first eight years of my life, a place in the shadow of the western outcrops of the Peak District and originally sustained by the mills, which had harnessed the fast-running water pouring down off the hills to drive its silk industry. There was so much water, in fact, that on the high ground around the town were reservoirs where the rain could be collected, stored and piped to our kitchen tap – for a small, but in our household, resented charge. My brother used to go sailing on the square-ended Rudyard Lake, just over the border in Staffordshire, while the rest of us went for 'runs' in my dad's Ford Zephyr to the Goyt Reservoir on the way to the Derbyshire spa town of Buxton.

If my mother believed free water was, like the air we breathe, akin to a human right, then Buxton takes that train of thought one stop further. It is one of the centres of the peculiarly Derbyshire custom of well-dressing, a practice rooted in the notion that not only is water free, it is a gift from God, or the gods, and that we therefore need to give thanks to this divine provider if we want supplies to continue uninterrupted. Once upon a time such a belief was the norm. Most Neolithic stone circles, including Stonehenge, feature an avenue leading away from them towards a water source. At Wilsford in Wiltshire, a deep well-shaft was found in the 1960s that has been dated back to the Bronze Age – 3,500 years ago. At the bottom were various devotional objects – thrown in, archaeologists suggest, to placate and pay homage to water gods as part of the water cult.

Christianity, up to and including medieval times, took over and remodelled many of these existing pagan rituals around water by the simple but effective device of turning the sites of worship into holy wells, to be dressed on saints' days, but that practice too slowly died out, seen as a distraction by the Protestant reformers, and eventually overtaken by industrialization and the march of technology. They swept away the reverence we once had for water. It no longer, for example, was seen as a source of healing. That was now the job of science and medicine. So the wells fell into neglect as, in the developed world at least, we became blasé about the clean water that comes readily out of our taps.

Everywhere, that is, except Buxton and a handful of other Derbyshire sites – Youlgreave, Tissington and Tideswell. There they maintained, more or less without interruption, the centuries-old tradition in summer months of well-dressing, placing next to ancient wells elaborate display panels of designs depicting biblical stories and made up of petals and leaves pushed into potters' clay. Quite why this custom survived in Derbyshire and not elsewhere is very hard to pin down.

A revival in well-dressing in the county towards the middle to late nineteenth century is well documented, led by Victorian antiquaries who saw in this ancient countryside practice a romantic escape from the grime and misery of the swelling industrial towns that were encroaching on the Peak District – Manchester to the west, Sheffield to the east, Derby and Nottingham to the south. It was a kind of mitigation for the worst excesses of urbanization that had drawn from the country to the towns the very people who used to make well-dressings.

Well-dressing had shrunk back again to about a dozen places by the 1950s, but thereafter – at precisely the point when my parents were taking me over to Buxton on outings – it started to blossom again. Today there are getting on for 80 towns and villages dressing their wells between May and August all over Derbyshire, with more joining in each year, some of them over the county boundaries into Cheshire and Staffordshire. To find out why this revival is taking place, I headed back to home ground one July weekend to visit two communities that have begun dressing their wells in recent years – one just inside Cheshire and the other in Derbyshire.

*   *   *

The south-eastern suburbs of Manchester stretch out along one busy, slightly shabby shopping street, lined with gloomy, self-important buildings that match the gloomy sky. The weather forecast on the car radio is still promising sunshine, a reasonable assumption for the time of year, but I wonder, as I reach over and switch it off, how long the tax-payer will continue paying for the staff at the Met Office to peer into crystal balls that regularly get it so spectacularly wrong about our changeable climate.

The names on the road signs ring bells, overheard in the re-telling of family stories that happened before I was old enough to be a conscious participant: there's one to Romiley, where my sister went to convent school, and another to Marple, where 'Mrs Doings from next door', as my father called her, moved after her husband died. There are, though, no real memories of the place, only a dislocated and vague affection.

It is just before I get to Compstall that there start to be brief green breaks between each cluster of houses and shops. Then, suddenly, the road is plunging down Compstall Brow into a steep-sided, wooded valley that the locals call, with considerable poetic licence, Little Switzerland. The gradient may have something in common with a ski-slope, but there are no chalets or white tipped peaks and not even a hint of Heidi.

Instead I spot the solid Victorian Anglican parish church of Saint Paul sheltering behind a leafy graveyard on my left, halfway down the hill, and pull into the car park. At the back of the plot, in the grounds of one of those big, handsome old vicarages that make you envy those material comforts that came with a vocation in ages past, is an ancient well, now overgrown. It is more of a spring, evidently, but in this neck of the woods wells, I am about to learn, don't have to be a circle of bricks round a deep shaft in the ground, with a bucket suspended over the top. The spot where underground water bubbles up through rocks can just as easily be labelled a well.

It was the presence of just such an outpouring in the vicarage garden that first led to talk in St Paul's, Compstall, of well-dressing. There was no history of doing it here in the past, but it does somehow make sense because of Compstall's reliance for its very existence on water. At the bottom of Compstall Brow, the River Etherow used to provide the get-up-and-go for a water wheel that, from the late eighteenth century, powered a cotton mill. 'Big Lily' was said to have been not just the largest of her kind in England, but the largest in the whole world, the sort of claim that carries with it an echo of those maps where half the world is coloured pink. Although made of iron, Big Lily (like the British Empire) did not endure, though the mill buildings themselves are still there as houses and workshops.

As I rummage for an umbrella in the back of the car, and toy with wearing Wellingtons, I try to think of the rain that is now falling as sacred rather than a nuisance. If I was in sub-Saharan Africa and not suburban Cheshire it might be easier. Yet, if scientists are to be believed, and I think they probably are on this one, levels of rainfall are soon once again going to be more than an excuse for a good old British moan about the weather. Global warming and rising sea levels threaten to leave great swathes of the planet as desert, and others, like ours, as cold and marshy. The superstitious and the fundamentalists would say that this looming catastrophe was a result of our failure to show appropriate reverence for water, or give thanks for its abundance to a higher power. 'If only it were that simple,' I think as I put the Wellingtons back in the car-boot and risk the puddles without them. But then perhaps the revival in well-dressing is one way, in the face of complex, scary science and the mammoth task of radically altering our behaviour, of trying to make it simple once more?

Over in the parish hall – the sort of utilitarian early twentieth-century building that I instinctively associate with episodes of *Dad's Army* – I seek out Pam Etherington-Smith, who last year brought well-dressing over the nearby border from Derbyshire to Compstall. The man collecting entrance fees on the door points her out immediately. Tall, capable and in her early sixties, she is good-humouredly setting up stalls for what looks like an indoor village fête. The well-dressing – which is to be blessed in half an hour – is to be the centrepiece of a community celebration.

'I'd wanted to do a well-dressing for a long time,' Pam explains as she guides me out of the hall, back down the slope, past the car park, and towards a corner of the churchyard that once used to house the upper mill pond but now is the site of the well-dressing panels. 'But I didn't know how. As you're about to see, its still far from perfect.' Why, though, did she want to do it? 'I think,' she replies, 'because we wanted to give thanks for the gift of water. I think we need to be much more aware of what is around us, creation, if you like, and stop doing things like pouring bleach down sinks and drains.'

She says it in such a matter-of-fact way, as if it is something everyone thinks. One archaeologist, Colin Burgess, has suggested that the original water cult developed in the Bronze Age because of climate change back then, with drier conditions making wells more important. So arguably there is a sense of history repeating itself in the growth of well-dressing right now. 'We certainly take it for granted and we shouldn't,' Pam replies when I voice the thought. 'We should treat it with respect and be grateful that we've got it.' She doesn't sound entirely convinced, and we walk on.

'Just tweak it up, Henry,' she calls out to an older man in a Barbour and cap, standing in front of the well-dressing. He's trying to reposition an overhanging branch from the tree that protects the dressing but which, under the weight of the downpour, is beginning to sag down and spoil the view. Pam is, it is becoming obvious, a practical, precise soul, not a willowy romantic harking back to a lost age of rural simplicity. She combines running the parish newsletter with teaching maths and swimming, as well as presiding over her family of five grown-up offspring and six grandchildren.

Henry dutifully stands back to let us see the fruits of the past week's labours by a group of around 16 volunteers, working in shifts in the parish hall. The wooden frame that surrounds the well-dressing is slightly taller than me – getting on for seven feet – and the scene it contains is divided like a triptych, with the larger central panel flanked by thinner ones on either side. The theme is taken from the Gospel of Saint John, where Jesus meets a Samaritan woman at a well and promises that 'whoever drinks the water that I give him will never be thirsty again. The water that I will give him will become in him a spring which will provide him with life-giving water and give him eternal life.'

It was the idea of water bringing life that appealed to the parishioners of Compstall, something tangible that they could identify with and unite behind. 'We've tried to base it on industry and water,' says Pam. 'The water was here. It brought

George Andrew and his family to Compstall to build the mill. They lived in the house opposite.' She gestures across the road.

I only have eyes, however, for the well-dressing. On such a dull, grey day, against such a vibrantly green backdrop, its pinks, yellows and blues have the same effect as unfurling a pile of colourful, exotic saris in the middle of a sober, middle England marketplace. In this carefully manicured corner of the Cheshire landscape, there is also something irresistible about the primitive nature of the design. A phrase from the Gospel passage is picked out in white petals – 'Take the water of life as a gift'. Around it, each section of the panel is carefully delineated by peppercorns and then the details are picked out with more petals, leaves and whatever other natural materials – as tradition demands – they have to hand. In times gone by, they would all have been locally grown or gathered, but in the twenty-first century the rule has been stretched to include natural materials available in the local supermarket. So there are a few lentils, and some dried peas and beans in a variety of colours, none of them obviously native species of this corner of Cheshire.

The original design was first drawn on a piece of paper, Pam explains, which was then laid over the clay panels. With pointed sticks, pushed through the paper into the clay, it was picked out and marked in outline. There followed the process of filling in the sections. Each petal is pushed in separately, one overlapping the next, like tiles on a roof, so that, in theory, the rain will flow straight off this outdoor display. The overall effect is a bit like painting by numbers on a grand and rather eccentric scale.

At the heart of the picture is Compstall Mill and Big Lily with water flowing through it, picked out in the sky-blue blooms of hydrangeas. In the top left and right corners are bees – sunflower petals and coffee beans alternating to make their stripes. And then there is the well – more in line with the stereotypical wishing-well than the spring behind the vicarage – with the sand around it rendered, Pam reveals, by mixing in a bit of out-of-date plaster.

'We've tried to base it on industry and water' –
the well-dressing in Compstall.

All the materials are held in place by the clay that is contained in the wooden frame, its dampness keeping the flowers from wilting for about seven days. 'We don't really puddle our clay like they do in other places,' Pam explains, getting technical. I look blank. She sighs. 'You remember when they built the canals?' Here, I recognize, is a woman with an interest in history. Local history in particular. Neither of us, I suggest, is of an age to remember them building the canals. She tuts. 'Do you know anything about canal building?' I shake my head. 'When the navvies dug the trench, they put special clay in and then sent a herd of cows down to trample it and so make a waterproof lining. The puddling in the clay panels is the same, but we don't use cows. We just pound it in. In some places they may do it with their feet, but there are nails inside this clay to hold it in place.' The image of a group of Cheshire villagers gathering in the church hall to dance in bare feet on a clay platform full of nails lingers longer than it should in my imagination.

There is, I have gathered from my reading, usually a hereditary element in well-dressing, skills passed down through the generations, usually in the female line. Had they called in more experienced well-dressers from Derbyshire to teach them the tricks of the trade? 'Not really,' Pam replies. 'They've been doing one over the hill at Holy Trinity, Gee Cross, for about nine years, so they were able to tell us something, but it was more from some classes a few of us went to on well-dressing in Stockport's Community Heritage Centre. We are still learning.'

So well-dressing is now being taught – another factor

'And is there honey still for tea?' – the well-dressing in
Swallow House Lane, Hayfield, based on a line from
'The Old Vicarage, Grantchester' by Rupert Brooke.

fuelling the revival. The teams of volunteer dressers at Comp-stall were, Pam reports, largely made up of the enthusiastic but untrained. And of more women than men – 'until we got to the heavy stuff of bringing it out and placing it here last night'. It must have taken them an eternity to complete because there are literally thousands of petals, peas and peppercorns. 'About a week,' she replies, bringing me back to earth.

Pam steps forward to press a sunflower petal in place that is in danger of falling off and exposing a naked bee. 'We put these in because Stuart and Caroline keep them locally. They live up on Werneth Low. That's the hill where I was born. In this part of the world a lot of the hills are called lows because they're not that high. At least that's where I'm assuming it comes from. Stuart and Caroline keep bees which come to the lime trees in the grove here on the edge of the graveyard when they're in flower. There are 12 trees – to represent the 12 apostles'.

It is estimated that around three-quarters of modern well-dressings still take a biblical theme – though to mark the Millennium, Derbyshire County Council wrote to organizing committees suggesting that they might consider other works of literature as their inspiration. Even if the origins of the practice are pagan, in places like Compstall well-dressing seems to be very much a churchy thing. And as Pam and I have been standing talking, the congregation has been slowly assembling on the edge of the car park in front of the panels. Last year, for their first well-dressing, they had 150, but Pam is worried the weather will put people off this time.

The clouds have, mercifully, dried off momentarily as the Revd Jane Brooke, priest-in-charge, joins us. We are going to be able to give thanks for water without being drowned in it. A young girl sets the ball rolling by playing a few notes on her flute. The service of blessing, Jane admits, is a bit mix and match. She has written the prayers herself.

Her admission reveals something of the curious relationship between well-dressing and organized religion. Even though well-dressings have been carried out under church auspices at places like Tissington for almost 700 years, there appears to be

no section in the Book of Common Prayer devoted to this particular ceremony. It has always been a kind of sideline, the
Church extending its community role to give an essentially
informal blessing to something that is as much part of the
seasons and the natural cycle of life in the countryside as
beating the bounds or giving thanks for the harvest.

'Loving God,' Jane intones, 'thank you for the water in this
place. Thank you for the old wells, which have provided water
to so many people in Compstall over the years. Thank you for
the water that drove the mill and provided work to the local
community.'

It's beginning to feel as if I am on a virtual tour of the area
and its historic sites. I look around at the congregation. Last
year's numbers have been exceeded. By my crude calculations,
there are 200 here, even in the rain – or break in the rain. At
this rate of growth, they will soon need a bigger arena. Or, as
in the case of other parvenus to the well-dressing habit, to
spread their panels around various sites in the village.

'Do the pagan roots of the well-dressing make Jane cautious
about giving the ceremony the Church's blessing?' I ask afterwards, as the crowd begins to break up. 'No,' she replies, 'I
don't feel uncomfortable because of the presence of the
Etherow, the water in this area, because water is from God,
and because of the enjoyment of the water. There's no problem
as long as we have something where we are saying thank you
to God too.' As an add-on, as it were.

Much the same logic, I suspect, inspired Victorian vicars to
participate in the nineteenth-century revival – just as allowing
the essentially pagan habit of bringing trees indoors in
December was allowed because it could be justified as a way of
marking Jesus's birth. What's the harm in a pagan practice if it
is given a Christian veneer? There has been, Jane reports, one
parishioner uncomfortable at the pagan undertones in well-
dressing, but hers has been a lone voice. And she's coming to
the fête in the hall afterwards, so it is hardly entrenched oppo-
sition. How does the vicar account for the current revival?
'Well, it's always been there. And we are doing it only because

someone was longing to do it and had energy to do it.' A nice tribute to Pam, but not, perhaps, sufficient of an explanation for why 200 people (between three and four times the usual Sunday congregation at St Paul's) have just gathered in a sodden car park. Last year, the novelty may have had something to do with it. But now?

Among those hanging back as people head up to the church hall is Henry. How involved was he in making the dressing? 'A little,' he replies – modestly Pam tells me subsequently. And what was the appeal? 'Well, it's a community thing, not a religious thing. It's doing the thing together. This is a decent little village. I've been here 36 years. There are still more sheep in this parish than people.' I'm still wondering if Henry is passing a social comment, or making a joke, given how built-up the road into Compstall has been, when he looks back at the panels, his handiwork, and smiles a contented smile. 'We had a terrible job putting those on.' He points to some white petals. 'And those coffee beans.' He shakes his head at the memory.

Back in the parish hall I meet Susan, who lives in Romiley. 'I'm retired,' she explains, 'and like going to well-dressings locally. I saw an article in the local newspaper about what was happening here and thought I'd like to see how they do them. It's been very interesting but very stressful. There are so many things you can't use. We've tried pasta, but with the damp, it goes soggy.' Is she a churchgoer? 'No, never. I just like local knowledge. I've lived here all my life. And Buxton's only 18 miles away. I still consider it local. People are getting more interested in old traditions.'

Her description is making me think of the American habit of communities getting together to make a quilt out of panels provided by individual members. There are the quilting bees – groups of (usually) women who will gather as they sew their panels – depicted in the 1995 film, *How to Make an American Quilt*, starring Maya Angelou, Winona Ryder and Anne Bancroft. And famously there is the giant AIDS Memorial Quilt, begun in 1987 as a way of grieving friends and relatives recording their loved ones at a time when death from AIDS carried a social stigma and made those left behind feel isolated and cast out of their communities.

Like these quilts, well-dressings are both an excuse for people gathering together in the face of society that can seem ever more fragmented, and a form of community folk art, traditional, anti-modern even. The Amish, the backward-looking American Christian denomination noted for their simple dress and plain lifestyles, are big quilters, often preferring black rather than 'worldly' red or yellow panels so as to make their output an expression of their austere religious philosophy.

I try out the theory on Pam. 'Well, we do laugh and joke as we are pushing the petals in,' she confirms, 'especially when they won't go flat. You should have been there for the insanity when we ran out of white petals and we couldn't find a chrysanthemum anywhere. Then I found some in the churchyard. Not off a grave, though I did look there first. Actually they're not chrysanthemums, but they did.'

She then adds, almost as an afterthought, an intriguing thought – that there was sometimes a meditative aspect to such a slow, labour-intensive task as colouring in the panels. The action of pushing all those petals into the clay would be, I can easily imagine, repetitive and, however good the company, occasionally boring when stretched over five or seven days. To keep on doing it, you would have, somehow, to find a way of transcending the mechanical detail of it. 'Think higher thoughts,' as we used to be taught at Sunday school.

One parallel tradition with well-dressing lies in how Christians, in centuries past, used to encourage themselves to think higher thoughts by walking round and round labyrinths (laid out on the pavement stones of great medieval cathedrals such as Chartres) or mazes (in monastery gardens or churchyards) as part of their Lenten observances. There is the connection with well-dressing that both use nature in worship – at least in the plants that make up the maze. And another in that sense of having a time of gruelling but mindless preparation before an act of worship or honouring. There was, of course, in such medieval observances none of our modern impulse, when confronted by a maze, of solving a mystery. The point was to do something with the body that left the mind (and spirit) free, rather like the act of making a well-dressing late into the night – as they have been in Compstall parish hall.

But labyrinths and mazes were often navigated alone. Well-dressing is a community thing. Does it, I ask Pam, go beyond a sense of local community to embrace a broader sense of identity? She thinks for a moment. 'Whenever I am asked for my nationality, I put "English". I know I'm not supposed to. I'm supposed to be British or European, or something. But I'm English first, aren't I? It's hard to be English because we don't have a traditional costume. Like the Scots have their kilt. And the Welsh have their hats. The Irish have their . . . You know what I mean. Ours has got lost in the mists of time. I think well-dressing is harking back to something that you can't get hold of. I like to have this connection going back with people in times gone by.'

As if to emphasize her point, the fête is now getting under way around us. The tea-urn is steaming, the tombola barrel turning, and homemade cakes going down a treat. A group of local schoolgirls gathers in the middle of the floor to entertain us with country dancing. All the elements are here of the jumble of images that pass today for authentic Englishness. As the troupe begins to weave in and out to the tune of 'The Blaydon Races' pumped out on the piano, the sun appears in the windows.

*   *   *

The border with Derbyshire is, as Pam has promised, just a few miles down the road. Whatever its recent history in places like Compstall, Cheshire can boast no enduring history of well-dressing (though curiously there was, in Victorian times, a separate but not dissimilar practice in the salt town of Nantwich in the south of the county of putting floral tributes on the brine-springs that brought the place prosperity). If you are trying to understand well-dressing, then Derbyshire is the only place to be in, so, under clearing skies, I head for the village of Hayfield in the High Peak.

It is longer in the tooth than Compstall at well-dressing, but still a relative novice with a history of just five years to its name. The traditional sites for well-dressing all lie in what locals call the White Peak – the upland areas of Derbyshire that are underlain by white limestone rocks. Limestone, quarried in the nineteenth century around Buxton, is porous and makes for dry valleys and poor soil. So wells that tapped underground water sources to nourish an often parched and barren topsoil were especially prized.

Wrapped round the White Peak to the west, north and east, like a horseshoe, is the Dark Peak – now officially called the High Peak to avoid causing offence. Here, the hills tend to be higher and wilder. The limestone plateau is covered by a layer of impervious millstone grit, so surface water is plentiful, leading to saturated moorland and peat bogs, and making wells more a tool of drainage than sustenance.

As the road climbs through the old textile-making town of New Mills and the clouds descend once more, I keep coming back to the same question. Why Derbyshire? With so many other wells, spas and springs around the country, so many other limestone areas where water is scarce, why has only this county continued to dress its wells over so many centuries? Why has this folklorish custom lived on when others – such as couples plighting their troth next to wells on Palm Sunday – have died out?

*   *   *

The process of first the Romans and then Christians super-imposing their beliefs on the pre-existing indigenous water worship is well documented. At sites such as Bath, the Romans took the cult they found there dedicated to the native goddess, Sulis – reputedly responsible for the thermal springs that had already made the place popular with bathers and those seeking a health cure – and overlaid her with their own deities, notably

Minerva (based, in turn, on the Greek Athena) who was goddess of medicine. The Romans' interest in such springs, however, was not only practical – their ability to yield cures and/or pleasure – but also spiritual. Seneca the Elder (54 BC to AD 39), the celebrated Roman writer and rhetorician, laid down that 'where springs or rivers flow, we should build altars or make sacrifices'.

Layer upon layer of ritual and belief was piled up when the Christian Church came along and assumed the mantle of a new Roman Empire in the fifth century. So, at the Second Council of Arles in 452, its leaders sent out instructions as to how clerics throughout Europe were to deal with the pagan practices they encountered. 'If in the territory of a bishop infidels light torches or venerate trees, fountains or stones, and he neglects to abolish this usage, he must know that he is guilty of sacrilege.'

Yet water was – and remains – sacred within Christianity, another example of its tendency to be the second-hand rose of religions, borrowing extensively from older traditions but claiming the result as its very own. Christians are baptized with water; they cross themselves with holy water when they enter churches; and at places of pilgrimage around the globe, Catholic Christians are encouraged to bathe in miraculous waters in the hope of being cured. Burgeoning early Christianity then had no difficulty at all in subsuming existing sites of water worship into its own structures and rituals. Up to the Reformation, in cities like Bristol for instance, all the major wells supplying the town were included in a formal religious procession that would include the Lord Mayor and the Council. With the Reformation such customs died out, damned as frivolous and ungodly in Protestant eyes.

So far, as clear as spring water. But whereas in the other parts of Britain the importance attributed to wells and springs (save in a very few and isolated cases) was diluted and washed away, in Derbyshire it continued. There are, of course, local factors in its survival. At Tissington, four miles north of Ashbourne, villagers claim that floral dressings on religious themes have been placed next to wells in thanksgiving since 1349, when the village escaped the Black Death because of the purity of its water sources. In the week around the annual unveiling of its well-dressings on Ascension Day, an estimated 50,000 visitors now come to Tissington. It has become one of the best-known tourist attractions in Derbyshire. Its longevity is wrapped up in the chocolate box good looks of the village itself and, in particular, with the fortunes of the village's age-old lords of the manor, the Fitzherberts of Tissington Hall, who have long run their family estate as a heritage industry, an historic backdrop for weddings, receptions and even ghost hunts.

At Tideswell (pronounced Tidsza), six miles from Buxton, another long-serving site for well-dressing, there was an ancient well that reportedly both ebbed and flowed, and was listed by the philosopher, Thomas Hobbes, as one of the 'Seven Wonders of the Peak' in his 1636 book of the same name. The well – which may or may not have given the village its name, depending on which authority you consult – subsequently dried up and long ago yielded its position as the major attraction to Tideswell's outsized fourteenth-century parish church, known as 'the Cathedral of the Peaks'.

And at Eyam towards Sheffield, the well on the outskirts of the village played a central role after plague struck in the 1660s when the village isolated itself to stop the disease infecting its inhabitants. The only supplies it received from the outside were left at the well and then washed in its purifying water to kill off any germs. Eyam is often quoted as the furthest point north the pestilence reached. By this account, the well helped turn the tide of disease and has been honoured ever since.

Yet none of these stories – colourful and persuasive as they are – can quite explain the history and survival of well-dressing throughout the county. Most accounts simply accept it and stop asking the question why. 'The origins are lost in antiquity,' says one visitor site. Which, as the writers probably know, is not just a cop-out, but also a draw. That element of mystery has its own attraction, as I've seen at Stonehenge. You can hang anything onto it without any real fear of contradiction.

So today well-dressings are being reinvented and rediscovered as a way of bringing communities together at a time of social dislocation. They provide both an ill-defined but strongly felt line of continuity with the past, and an imprecise expression of Englishness when national identity is uncertain. Part of the mix throughout these various twists and turns, however, has always been some element of the spiritual. What happens to well-dressing when, in line with our secular times, that is removed? In Hayfield, I am about to find out.

*   *   *

'It'll be a joint Anglican–Methodist blessing,' says Lynne Bagshaw, one of the organizers of Hayfield's nine well-dressings. A blonde-haired mother of grown-up children, warm without being gushing, she's bent over a final panel, pushing a loose petal into the clay with the arm of her glasses. These are finishing touches. Tomorrow, after a week of assembly, the well-dressings are officially unveiled. 'So the blessing is a part of it. And it's a community thing. That's Christian enough.'

There's almost an 'isn't it?' at the end of the sentence. Almost, but not quite. Hayfield's well-dressings are among that minority in Derbyshire that don't take their inspiration from the Bible. Or religion. Nor, unusually, do they bother much with local themes. They're both pretty secular and pretty far flung. Last year it was Hans Christian Andersen, Danish writer of fairy tales. In their first year – five summers ago – they tackled the Celts, which does, I suppose, potentially have spiritual overtones. And the theme this time round is 'Poetry and Verse'. One dressing is based on 'The Owl and the Pussycat', another 'The Pied Piper', and a third 'The Song of Hiawatha', but there's not a Derbyshire poet among them, or a verse from the Good Book.

We're standing in a lock-up garage in the old part of Hayfield, all narrow streets and handsome, plain houses of honey-coloured stone. The River Sett is rushing by outside, pouring brownish water off slopes that lead up to Kinder Scout, the peat moorland plateau popular with walkers, the highest point in the county at over 2,000 feet. The well-dressers' HQ, one of six venues they use for 'wells-in-the-making' (all garages except a scout hut and the vestry of the Methodist chapel), is right next door to the Royal Hotel, which isn't half as grand as it sounds. Few of the dressers who have been working here the past week, Lynne reports, have particularly strong links with the church. 'St John's Methodist Church on the other side of the by-pass has its own flower festival that coincides with ours,' she says, even-handedly, 'and there will be cream teas at St Matthew's [the Anglican parish church] tomorrow.'

There is no tension there, just an assumption that the two things are basically separate. Which means that Hayfield has avoided the fate of Eyam where, in September 2006, the local vicar in this plague village, the Revd Andrew Montgomerie, refused to bless one of the three wells there because it featured the 'green man', what he took to be a pagan god of nature, essentially the same creature as Jack-in-the-Green who danced so lustily at Stonehenge. The vicar was arguably being optimistic in thinking that, after centuries of intermingling, he could separate out the threads of paganism, Christianity and community enthusiasm, but he still tried.

In the coming week, Lynne and some of the other organizers will be taking visitors on walking tours of their dressings. 'We've two coachloads of 25 booked in,' chips in Mary. Hayfield may be somewhere without much economic purpose since the decline of the paper, cotton and calico mills that once shaped it, but it is, it becomes apparent as the team talk me through their home turf, a place whose 3,000 inhabitants (who include commuters into Manchester and second homers) work hard to provide it with a new identity. It has an impressive record of community activity, organizing a May Queen Festival, a Sheepdog Trials and Country Show, and the Lantern Pike Fell-Running Race. It even had its own three-day

'The Owl and the Pussy Cat' at the Gospel Well in Hayfield.

international jazz festival from 1983, until complaints about the disruption caused by crowds of visitors caused it to be cancelled in 1989. Some still mourn the manner of its passing.

Isn't the garage with its single bare electric light bulb a bit inhospitable, I wonder? The weather outside isn't improving, and this high up it has turned chilly. 'No,' Lynne dismisses the thought. 'And we like it here because passers-by just drop in to help if they've time,' adds Mary. 'They all know we are here now. And once people get started, they love it. And keep coming back.' As if to prove her point, a face appears round the garage door. Rose ends up coming in and rolling up her sleeves.

Like Compstall, Hayfield had no tradition of giving thanks for water before this enthusiastic bunch of volunteers got going. If anything, being in the Dark Peak it has too much water rather than too little. What first gave Lynne the idea, she explains, was walking past the neglected well in Valley Road that had once served a terrace of Victorian workers' cottages. 'I'd lived in that terrace and knew about the well, but it had always been behind a locked gate or overgrown. So I thought, why not do something about it?'

She talked to a few friends and they decided to hold a meeting at the Royal to discuss the possibility of doing a well-dressing. They were quite prepared for no one to show up. In the end between 40 and 50 turned out. They had touched a nerve. Were there people among them who had experience of making dressings in other parts of Derbyshire? The women in the garage look around at each other, trying to remember. 'We did go and see how others did it,' Lynne reports. 'We still do, but we feel now that ours here in Hayfield are as good as any others in Derbyshire.' In well-dressing there is, it seems, another outlet for civic pride, local rivalries and competition, more usually channelled through the village cricket team or the scouts' five-a-side soccer tournament.

The claim to have reached, in five short years, the standard that has taken Tissington and Tideswell more than five centuries to perfect is a bold one and needs testing. Lynne, Mary and Rose down tools and give me a sneak preview of their walking tour. First stop is 'Hiawatha' on Bank Street, just off the main street, based on American poet Henry Wadsworth Longfellow's 1855 poem 'The Song of Hiawatha'. This elaborate panel sits next to what might better be described as a culvert rather than a well. Hayfield piles up the slopes on either side of the River Sett, and Bank Street Well is a great rectangular slab of stone, set in a retaining wall that holds up one of the terraces of houses that line the hillside. Today it is dry,

'Hiawatha' at Bank Street Well, Hayfield.

but during heavy downpours it directs the flow of surface water off the hill down the street and into a drain. Before a reservoir was built up on Kinder Scout in 1911, Hayfield flooded regularly.

Part of the pleasure of this modern incarnation of well-dressing seems to be the ingenuity required to find suitable materials to make up the designs that meet the criteria of being natural. For Lynne, it is a year-long task, keeping her eyes open for anything that might come in useful. 'We've used camomile for Hiawatha's tunic, parsley for the foliage, rosehip for the costume decorations and crushed brick for deer,' she says. Mary's face darkens. 'Does brick count as natural?' she questions. 'Its made of clay, isn't it?' Lynne reassures her.

Lynne and Mary at Valley Road Well, inspiration for them
taking up well-dressing.

It probably won't, however, wilt and die as quickly as many
of the other ingredients. How long do the dressings last?
'Usually about a week?' Lynne estimates. 'No more.' And do
they remain untouched? 'Well last year, a pair of hiking boots,
which we'd placed in front of one display, went missing, but
otherwise we've had no problems. They're left alone until they
die and then we come and move them.'

That transitory element in well-dressing is important. If it
wasn't, then Lynne and her colleagues could just as easily turn
graffiti artists or design great murals from the block ends of the
terraced streets that climb up the hillside in Hayfield. That
really would be a statement. Well-dressings, by contrast, in spite
of the local pride they clearly encourage, are essentially rather
humble. You work hard on them, they blossom briefly in public
places, and then they are swept away until next year, like the
cycles of agriculture, only on a small scale. And like the cycles of
life – on an even smaller scale. Everything must pass, and these
panels – flamboyantly built not to last – remind us of that.

That transitory quality links the well-dressing panels to other forms of community art around the globe, such as sand-painting among Native Americans, Tibetan monks and Aboriginals. All make, as part of an age-old community ritual, religious or healing pictures out of naturally coloured sands and stones, often coloured using flower pollen or powdered roots to add tone. The Navajo, in the south-western United States, for instance, then ritually destroy their sand-paintings of the Yeibicheii – or 'holy people' – within 12 hours. In some parts of Latin America, this ancient practice – whose origins remain obscure – has been incorporated within Christianity. So in Mexico, Dia de los Muertos – originally an Aztec festival, but now integrated into All Saints' Day and All Souls' Day (1 and 2 November in the Christian calendar) – is celebrated by decorating the streets with sand paintings that are afterwards swept away.

In Hayfield, any overt religious impulse behind well-dressing may have been lost, but there remains, unexamined but undeniably there, that spiritual element of reflecting on the mysteries of life and death as the petals in the clay decay and rot.

As we walk on and work our way round all nine Hayfield wells, we keep bumping into the same faces, following the same route which regularly doubles back on itself. It's part street theatre, part community ritual, part promenade. Some of the faces are familiar to Lynne and her team, others strangers, clutching one of the maps of the well-dressings that are available all round Hayfield, thanks to the sponsorship of local businesses – another twenty-first-century take on the custom. But everyone stops to talk, share observations, praise the handiwork. I try to see it too as a kind of local pilgrimage, something akin to the processions of old that would have been made to the wells on saints' days; but in the avowedly secular context of Hayfield's reinvention of well-dressing, it is perhaps a step too far.

4

Walsingham

Sinne is wher our Ladie sate,
Heaven turned into hell.
Sathan sittes wher our Lord did swaye
Walsingham oh farewell.

From a ballad attributed to Philip Howard,
Reformation martyr (1557–95)

It must be 25 years since I last picked up a hitch-hiker. Or two: computer programmers on their way to Devon, if I remember correctly. Soon afterwards I read a gruesome newspaper story about a dismembered driver, and that put me off letting thumb-waving strangers into my car ever again. But Walsingham has evidently softened me.

It's early August and I'm heading back into this north Norfolk village after registering for the annual 'New Dawn in the Church' conference, held in a farmer's field full of marquees directly opposite the Slipper Chapel, a fourteenth-century staging post that once marked the last leg of the Pilgrims' Way to the medieval Marian shrine of Walsingham. On the grass verge, I spot a middle-aged woman wearing a bright red anorak and peach-coloured trousers, making the traditional hitch-hiker's hand gesture. I know at once she is a fellow New Dawn delegate by the blue wallet hanging by a ribbon around her neck.

And anyway, why else would she be walking along this particular country lane? It must, I suppose, go somewhere, but the only people who appear to use it are those coming or going between the Slipper Chapel and the centre of Walsingham – more properly Little Walsingham, though perversely it is bigger than its near neighbour, Great Walsingham.

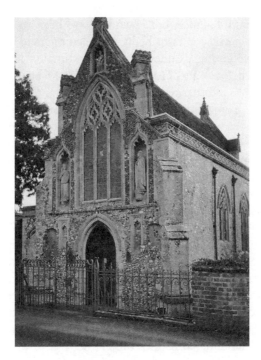

The Slipper Chapel
on the outskirts of Walsingham.

Somehow it feels wrong not to stop and offer this hitch-hiker a lift, as if I will be violating the fellowship that I have just signed up for in the marquee, albeit making clear that I will be only an observer. 'How much do I owe you?' I'd asked as I was given my own blue wallet necklace. 'We don't make any charge,' the elderly woman behind the desk had reassured me with a smile, 'but Jesus will tell you what you should give as a donation.' Such casual references to Jesus, even this far into my pilgrimage, continue to unsettle me. 'In my country,' a Kenyan missionary who had come over to save Manchester once told me, 'everyone knows the name of Jesus and his story. But in your country, many people I meet only know Jesus as a swear word.'

Put on the spot in the registration tent, I had puzzled to myself whether Jesus didn't have better things to do in a world tortured by inequality, injustice and war than keep track of the size of my bank balance, but it would have been rude to say it out loud when everyone was being so welcoming. So I'd paid up – £20 in case you're wondering what I estimated Jesus would put me down for – and instantly felt guilty at being parsimonious. Which is another reason why I pull up for the hitch-hiker.

'Are you from New Dawn?' she asks cautiously, peering short-sightedly in through the open passenger-door window. She must have read the same stories as I had in the papers. It doesn't seem like a time to start making fine distinctions – angels dancing on pinheads and all that – so I answer 'Yes', though lingering slightly on the 's'. She apparently misses the nuance, blossoms into a grin and gets in, bare ankles first.

She's in her late fifties and fills the car instantly with the whiff of cigarettes. 'Is this your first time?' she asks. So she did register that sibilant note of uncertainty in my voice. 'Yes,' I reply, repeating it, and peering ahead with exaggerated concentration at the narrow lane. 'And yours?' We are now even because I know what her answer is going to be. 'Oh no. I've been coming for years. Lots of us have. This is like a family gathering. I wouldn't dream of missing it.'

It is quite a claim, but one she is happy to unpack without any further probing. 'The Holy Spirit is here,' she explains in the same matter-of-fact voice she might use to tell me that the hedgerows we are driving past are green or that the summer breeze is warm and pleasant through the open car window. 'And not elsewhere?' I probe. 'You can see him here.' I am just registering the masculine pronoun when she adds: 'If you are willing to look', and shoots a look at me.

As I write it down now, her challenge sounds rather like the sort of childlike imperative uttered by those unabashed fundamentalists who have the nerve to ring your front bell at eight o'clock on a Saturday morning and greet you in your dressing-gown with an invitation to be friends with Jesus. And are usually rewarded, at our place anyway, with a quickly closed, if not slammed, door. But here, in my car, in a Norfolk country lane that has been a pilgrimage route for centuries, her evangelizing is somehow harder to shut out.

My passenger is now staring ahead again, smiling at the

world and to herself. Point made. Her unsullied eyes are fixed on the horizon as she explains she is popping back into Walsingham village to pick up from her bed-and-breakfast a book that she has promised to lend someone at New Dawn. 'They've been coming from the start too,' she adds. I am evidently being let in on a secret.

I drop her, as requested, near the newsagents. After she has got out and I'm driving away, I watch her, in my wing mirror, hover until she thinks I've gone and then go in for her nicotine fix. Even this worldly weakness, though, can't quite snuff out her impact.

*   *   *

Desiderius Erasmus didn't take to Walsingham when he visited in 1512, though he returned to take a second look in 1524. 'Falsingham', he labelled it in *A Pilgrimage for Religion's Sake* (*Peregrinatio religionis ergo*). The Dutch Christian humanist was, in the early decades of the sixteenth century, one of the leaders of the movement within Catholicism that wanted the Church to reform itself and so heal the rift that had opened up with Martin Luther. And part of that reforming process, Erasmus believed, was to 'clean up' abuses at places such as Walsingham so as to answer Luther's specific criticisms of the trade in relics and the commercial activities of monks at sites of pilgrimage. Erasmus was therefore horrified by the legion of salesmen he encountered in Walsingham who were attempting to sell a square of tattered cloth by passing it off as the Virgin Mary's veil, or a bottle of white liquid as her breast milk. This wasn't what Catholicism was really about, he raged.

At the time, Walsingham was the Lourdes of its day, the grandest of Marian shrines in Europe, visited by every English king from Edward I to Henry VIII (who came in 1519 to thank God for the birth of his son, Henry). Its story as a sacred place had begun in 1061, before the Norman Conquest, when the local lady of the manor, Richeldis de Faverche, a widow by some accounts, deeply devout by all, claimed to see a vision of the Virgin Mary. Christ's mother, Lady Richeldis reported, made only one request of her – to build an exact replica of the Holy Family's house in Nazareth at Walsingham.

Quite why Jesus's mother would have wanted this is unexplained. The sort of logical explanations that twenty-first-century minds demand wouldn't have been required in medieval times. For those of faith, it was enough that Mary had come and asked. Whatever her request, however odd it may sound, it would be honoured. And devotion to the 'Holy House' was not unique to Walsingham. What was thought to be the original family home of Joseph, Mary and Jesus in Nazareth had been later subsumed into a basilica, built by the Roman Emperor Constantine after he converted to Christianity in the fourth century. Catholic legend (though not official teaching) holds that, in 1291, to avoid the 'Holy House' being damaged in the battles of the Crusaders to recapture the Holy Land, it was miraculously picked up and transported by angels, via a three-year stop-over in present-day Croatia, to the Italian town of Loreto, where it became a site of pilgrimage and remains so to this day, a small house within a vast and much-visited church.

Walsingham's replica 'Holy House' was already in situ 200 years before Loreto trumped it with what it claimed was the real thing. Once completed, next to two wells believed to have healing powers, the Walsingham Holy House was surrounded by an abbey complex that grew up as this remote spot in north Norfolk, ten miles inland from the sea, attracted ever larger numbers of the faithful, many of them walking there along established pilgrim routes to 'Little Nazareth'.

Reading Erasmus's account of his trips to the shrine in the sixteenth century reminded me of a teenage visit I had made with my Christian Brother teachers to Lourdes in 1980. Like Erasmus in Walsingham, I found the actual sanctuary of the French shrine moving and the faith of visitors palpable, but I recoiled from the traders outside the main gates with their rosary beads, bottles of holy water and Our Lady flick-knives. These pointed to a cancer at the heart of contemporary Catholicism, a commercialization and a vulgarization of something that should stand out against such tendencies, and so put me off visiting such places ever after. Until, that is, I came to Walsingham.

The simony of present-day Lourdes has no parallel in modern Walsingham. The merchants that Erasmus bemoaned are long gone, though it was Henry VIII's Dissolution of the Monasteries in 1537, rather than the actions of any reforming pope, that swept them away. Prince Henry's birth in 1519 had brought his father, Henry VIII, to Walsingham to give thanks. Had the child lived, Walsingham's history might have been different – along with England's – but the infant's subsequent death and the failure of Catherine of Aragon to provide her husband with another son and heir saw the King turn against Rome (though in some accounts, on his deathbed Henry commended his spirit to Our Lady of Walsingham). Walsingham Abbey and its vast priory church were destroyed, along with many other ecclesiastical centres.

The high street, where I drop my hitch-hiker, is hardly thronging with people, even in mid-summer. There is a small Post Office, an ice-cream parlour, an ethical clothes boutique and a couple of modest gift shops. Their windows may be stuffed with tat – laminated pictures of the Virgin Mary, rosary beads, devotional cards and the like – but it is not the worst sort of tat. Which is no great loss – though the idea of being able to buy a bottle of something reputed to be the Virgin Mary's breast milk is so ghoulish and psychologically bizarre, it is almost fascinating.

The centre of Walsingham excites architectural historians, for many of its medieval buildings survived during the long hibernation of the village after the Reformation when it became yet another centre for local farms. What has been lost, though, is almost all of the medieval church architecture that Erasmus would have admired. What was not wrecked by Henry's henchmen was left to crumble for nigh on five centuries. The Slipper Chapel, for instance, was variously used as a poor house, a forge, a cowshed and a barn. Its survival is the only miracle I witness at Walsingham.

It was rescued in 1863, all but intact under a protective coating of straw and animal droppings, by another devout local gentlewoman, Charlotte Pearson Boyd. She was an Anglican at the time, though in the High or Anglo-Catholic wing of the Church of England that admired much of what Rome stood for – especially the historical continuity it represented back via the first apostles to Christ. Subsequently, she converted to Catholicism and so it was to her new church that she gifted the Slipper Chapel. She took part in the first post-Reformation Marian pilgrimage in 1897.

Behind a grand set of black wooden gates on the high street lie the grounds of a solid, honey-coloured Georgian hall owned by the Meath-Bakers, descendants of the founders of Barclays Bank. In the middle of the side lawn stands the enormous and gravity-defying 'Lonely Arch', almost all that is left of the east window and wall of the medieval priory church. It reaches up to the heavens, as was the way with architecture when it was built, every spire stretching to reach out to paradise in imitation of Jacob's Ladder. The sheer scale of it gives some idea of the size of the monastery that was established here by Augustinian canons in 1130.

In the early decades of the twentieth century, following that first post-Reformation pilgrimage, a modest (in comparison with past glories) revival washed over Walsingham. As well as seasonal Catholic activity around the Slipper Chapel (there was still no resident Catholic priest), the Revd Alfred Hope-Patten arrived in 1921 as the local Church of England vicar and set about encouraging like-minded Anglicans to restore the practice of Marian pilgrimages to Walsingham. He spent the rest of his life here, erecting a series of buildings to receive pilgrims, including another replica of the Holy House – or, more precisely, a replica of the original replica.

Hope-Patten had ambiguous feelings about Roman Catholics. 'On the one hand, he admired Rome from afar, particularly Rome as demonstrated in Belgium and Austria,' writes his biographer, Michael Yelton. 'On the other hand, he had next to no contact with, or even knowledge of, Roman Catholics in this country.' Hope-Patten claimed on several occasions to have been wooed by Rome, with the promise of being named a monsignor (a papal honour) if he agreed to 'come over' and run a Catholic parish in Walsingham, but he had, he reported, declined. So the Anglican shrine in the centre of the village, and the Catholic one at the Slipper Chapel, operated separately – and still do.

Miss Pearson Boyd had also tried to buy the ruins of the priory church from the owners of the big house, but failed. So no denomination has been able to claim as its own this prize relic of Walsingham's past. For most of the year, the Lonely Arch stands as a monument to the faith of past ages rather than a living place of worship. Indeed, for many visitors its appeal is historical and secular – especially in the early spring when thousands turn up to walk in the snowdrop woods that surround it. The fact that Anglican and Catholic presences in Walsingham remain separate may indeed harden the hearts of secular visitors. They look at the remains of a church ruined by past religious divisions and then witness them living on in the village to this day.

*   *   *

I return at ten o'clock on the morning after registering and join the estimated 3,000 New Dawners gathering in bright sunshine outside the main tent for a scheduled rosary walk from the Slipper Chapel into Walsingham itself. I am momentarily tempted to stop off and buy some rosary beads in one of the religious gift shops in the village – but then dismiss the thought. They will be an impediment to observing objectively. And anyway, as a child I had possessed countless sets, usually in black plastic, though the ones that stand out in my memory were turquoise and crushed into a small see-through case that sat for years collecting dust on top of my chest of drawers. Rosary beads were, back then, standard prizes for good Catholic children at school and parish functions, or Easter gifts from maiden aunts.

It is not only a sign of my own carelessness that these keepsakes are now misplaced. Rosary beads have become an endangered species in most Catholic churches, especially in the hands of anyone under 60. Many younger churchgoers won't, for example, know the details of the three sets of five 'mysteries' – sorrowful, joyous and glorious – that are traditionally part of 'saying' the rosary. And they probably wouldn't be able to match my remaining manual dexterity, learnt all those years ago, in working my way round the chain, a bead at a time, each representing a mystery and each requiring the recital of one 'Our Father', ten 'Hail Marys' and a final 'Glory Be'.

I walk around the farmer's field trying to blend in. Through the open flaps of the main marquee I spot a group of twenty-something musicians rehearsing a liturgical song on a small stage in one corner. The sound of acoustic guitars, simple harmonies and upbeat choruses puts me in mind of the anthem about 'the dawn of the age of Aquarius' from the late 1960s musical *Hair* – though here the lyrics are God-centred (and the performers have their clothes on). There is a stagey exuberance to the rehearsal – with the singers closing their eyes and stretching out their hands, palms upwards at shoulder height, as if waiting to catch a gift dropped down from heaven, or from the rafters of the tent.

As they repeat the chorus again and again, my gaze wanders round the makeshift church. In the centre, next to a formidable bank of black loudspeakers, two young women in brightly coloured T-shirts, bare legs and floral patterned wellies sit with their heads bowed. Around them a group of older folk, dressed simply, several sporting large crucifixes but none of them in obvious clerical gear, are praying and laying hands on the pair. Despite the public setting, this is an intimate moment and I turn away.

New Dawn is an organization firmly rooted in the charismatic branch of modern Christianity, which sees everywhere the presence of the Holy Spirit, the third (and often neglected) part of the Holy Trinity. The gifts (or charisms) of the Spirit, according to the Acts of the Apostles, came down on Jesus's disciples on the first Pentecost Sunday in the form of tongues of fire. One minute these frightened and dispirited fishermen, terrified by the death, resurrection and ascension into heaven of their leader and their consequent abandonment, were contemplating returning to the Sea of Galilee and their nets. The next they were able to talk confidently before large crowds in languages that all their hearers could understand. This 'gift of tongues' was accompanied by the 'gift of healing'. Just as Jesus had healed the sick and wounded by laying his hands on them, his apostles could now go out and cure.

The charismatic revival movement that started in the 1960s has long had a difficult relationship with Catholicism. The two stand, by and large, at opposite ends of the liturgical spectrum. Many in the Roman hierarchy remain sceptical of the emotional disinhibition of charismatic services, the touchy-feely nature of their liturgies and the movement's empowerment of the laity. But New Dawn exists within the fold, albeit at its periphery, facilitating a spiritual exploration usually unavailable in most parish churches. This is its twenty-first annual gathering at Walsingham.

In the field, young and old, male and female – though many more women with grey hair than anyone else – gather in one long line behind a statue of Our Lady of Walsingham that waits, surrounded by flowers and perched on a bier, ready to be hoisted up and carried at the head of the procession into the village. By one of those extraordinary coincidences, the first face I latch onto in the crowd is that of an old schoolfriend who I last saw when he went on to train for the Catholic priesthood at the age of 18. He's in civvies, but immediately identifiable as a cleric. It is something about the utilitarian cut of his cloth, its muted colours and the way he looks so uneasy in his blue open-neck shirt and black suit trousers.

Brian was, I think, the only vocation from our year – despite the many retreat days we went on, hosted by priests gushing with charm and utterly unlike our monk teachers. Their bonhomie always ran a bit short, though, towards the end of the programme, when they would hand out cards. 'Tick one of the following boxes. I do feel I have a vocation. I don't feel I have a vocation. I would like to talk about it more before expressing a view.' They would hover close at hand as those they had identified as hopefuls picked up their pens. Once or twice I knew I was in the frame until I plucked up the courage, under such scrutiny, to make my mark next to the 'No' option. Now, I would opt for more talking – about, for instance, the notion of vocation that isn't wrapped up in ordination.

Brian never appeared to have any doubt back then that God

was calling him, for which, I blush to remember, he was often teased in the playground. That and a mild walking tic that gave him an odd, swinging gait, which is still there as I watch him moving easily among fellow delegates. I make my way over to reintroduce myself. He is immediately friendly. If he remembers those schoolboy torments, they have been offered up and long forgotten.

What is it about Walsingham that has drawn him here? 'It's New Dawn,' he replies. 'There's something happening here that I haven't experienced elsewhere.' Not even in his parish? 'No,' he laughs, with self-deprecating honesty, 'but I have come with a group of parishioners.' And what is the something happening? 'The Spirit in action,' he says. There is that word again.

Before we can get any further in decoding it, Brian is called away to put on his vestments. New Dawn may be democratic in blurring the distinction between clergy and laity as leaders, but it has a streak of traditionalism running through it. And if priests are going to lead the procession, they need to look like priests.

Perhaps it is this respect that the ordained ministry still – just about – commands in Catholicism that has given Brian his obvious self-confidence, so lacking when he was a schoolboy. Or perhaps it just comes with age and a job he enjoys. But here he looks absolutely at home. Which is more than I can say for myself as I loiter, smiling as invitingly as I can as groups assemble around me ready for the procession.

Finally someone takes the bait, an older man in a black-and-white herringbone tweed jacket. 'I'm Myles Dempsey,' he begins. He is the founder, he explains, of New Dawn. 'I started it with £20,' he recalls.

In the excitement of the first wave of charismatic renewal reaching Catholicism in the late 1960s and early 1970s, Dempsey had joined a charismatic prayer group in London's Soho. It was the start of a commitment that led him and his wife, in the mid-1980s, to set up in Greenwich, south London, a residential community for others in the Catholic charismatic renewal movement called Prince of Peace. In 1985, he was on a visit to Ars in France – famous for its nineteenth-century curé, Saint John Vianney, and a draw for charismatics because

Vianney was said to have had the gift of tongues. 'I was simply overwhelmed there by the power of the Spirit,' Dempsey recalls, 'and I found myself asking why we don't have somewhere similar in Britain. That was when I heard God speaking to me – "New Dawn and Walsingham", he said. I hardly knew Walsingham then. I'd only been here once. At first I wasn't sure and I even thought of doing it in Birmingham, but we were guided here. And it has grown. We had 800 in our first year, 1987. The power of the Spirit has made it grow.'

The Spirit seems, in this worldview, to be at the heart of anything that cannot be easily explained. Logically, in secular, sceptical times when Mass attendance is declining, a Catholic gathering at Walsingham should not be thriving. That it is turns logic on its head. There are several reasons a dispassionate observer might suggest for this counter-intuitive success – the tangible succour it offers to people searching beyond the bounds of traditional, institutional, Mass-on-Sunday Christianity; the particular exuberant and uninhibited qualities of its liturgies; the camaraderie that exists among regulars; that sense of finding like-minded individuals in a world and a Church that is otherwise hostile or indifferent to charismatic renewal. But such analysis is not the favoured approach of New Dawn. It prefers a simple answer for why this annual event is booming: the Spirit.

The procession in front of us is finally starting to move. Dempsey excuses himself. I wait a moment, trying to find the right place to attach myself to the line. I ask a group of women in their sixties if I can tag along with them as we begin to filter out of the field and into the lane, following the statue of Our Lady of Walsingham. They nod their assent. I'd imagined that on the rosary walk there would be the chance to chat and listen to the experiences of these contemporary pilgrims on this ancient road; but the rosary, I should have remembered, doesn't leave much room for small talk. It demands that your lips are always moving in praise of God, Mary and the Holy Trinity.

The members of my group all have their beads ready in their hands and are already praying out loud as we go through the gate. The grass ledges between the hedges and the tarmac road are steep banks and my immediate experience of the procession is of being funnelled, geographically and in my thoughts. The hum of prayers hovers over our heads like a lid on this strange world I have entered.

Quickly a pattern emerges. Each group has a leader – planned or not, I can't tell – and that leader announces one of the mysteries after which everyone in the set immediately behind him or her chants in unison their 'Our Father', 'Hail Marys' and 'Glory Be'. And then, without so much as a pause for breath or a gulp of water, it's on to the next mystery. The rosary is dedicated to the Virgin Mary and our group is getting through the 'joyful' mysteries of her life – Annunciation, Visita-tion, Nativity, taking Jesus to the Temple, losing and then finding Jesus at the Temple – at a cracking pace. At the end of each batch of five mysteries, we all sing a chorus of 'Ave Maria', though as we make our way down the lane and my ears grow accustomed to the overlapping sounds of each group, I realize that some are singing Mary's hymn to a different tune.

Even within our group, the words of the set pattern of prayers are not always in synch on every lip. Different accents can be picked out. There is a line of Irish voices, three older women in anoraks to my right, rushing ahead vocally, though trailing slightly on their pins. They pray in harmony with each other, intonation flattened in the interests of speed. Then, away to my left, I can hear some Brummie vowels, their source a younger woman in white blouse and heavy duty sandals, seemingly obliv-ious to everything around her. Up ahead of me, there are a couple of northern, possibly Lancashire, lilts provided by a well-ironed couple in their fifties, walking hand in hand, rosaries working simultaneously through the fingers of their free hands. Which, of our group, leaves only the two teenagers, in crumpled polo shirts and shorts, marching rather than walking, lips moving but, to my ears, with no distinctive sound emanating.

And, of course, there's me, no longer just an observer. When I first start joining in I am self-conscious, saying the words to myself, but leaving my vocal chords untroubled. This gradu-ally grows into a whisper as the memories of the central place of the rosary in my Catholic education trickle back. Finally, as we used to in the Christian Brothers' chapel. And rather enjoying it, though whether it is just nostalgia or something more, I can't tell.

This is, I decide, Gregorian chant for the masses – the familiar words of prayers indistinct in an overall sound that envelopes, soothes and carries you beyond. Beyond what, I was never sure, and remain unclear. You are meant, I was taught, to focus on each mystery rather than the actual words you are saying. 'The Carrying of the Cross', announces our leader, a balding man in waterproof trousers and a shirt that might have belonged to a Scout leader. I struggle to meditate on the details of the Via Dolorosa and find my feeble and worldly mind wandering to weigh up my surroundings.

The lane is utterly deserted but for our posse of pilgrims. No cars are tucked into its designated passing places as we troop by. Despite the absence of onlookers, we are, however, still participating in the kind of public demonstration of faith that is extremely rare in this country nowadays. In the 'Catholic' nations of Europe, such processions are a much more familiar sight. In Britain, however, the Reformation made us cautious of such emotional displays, nailing our faith colours to the mast. They used to go against the Protestant temperament. They still do, but now that is overlaid by a secular orthodoxy and the fear of standing out from the crowd as 'religious'. Slip quietly into church on a Sunday and it is your own business. Nobody need know or question you about it. But take part in a public procession behind a statue and you are inviting cross-examination and pigeon-holing as being different or odd.

I remember once interviewing the novelist and biographer, Peter Ackroyd, a cradle Catholic who had long ago detached himself from the Church of his birth, about his book on Thomas More, one of the martyrs of the English Reformation. 'Have you ever wondered what Britain would have been like if it had remained Catholic?' he mused. It was around the time of the death of Diana, Princess of Wales, and Ackroyd suggested, in answer to his rhetorical question, that the public outpouring of grief and the shrines of flowers that had been heaped outside her home could indicate a long-buried Catholicism resurfacing in our national psyche.

Rosary processions might also be much more common if, as Ackroyd had briefly imagined, Britain was still a Catholic country. But it isn't, and even here in Walsingham, arguably a place where that Catholic sensibility is buried in a shallower grave than elsewhere, the sight of 3,000 people following a statue of Our Lady up the high street, mumbling prayers and bursting into song, is enough to turn heads and prompt quizzical glances. The police are on hand to divert the traffic as we emerge from the side lane to the Slipper Chapel and onto the main drag that runs through Walsingham. Two workmen waiting impatiently in a white van lean out of the windows and stare unabashed. My fellow pilgrims are too wrapped up in their devotions to notice, but I meet the men's eyes and see in them puzzlement and mild scorn. By association I have stepped over some boundary but can detect no instinct in me to retreat.

On a few special occasions, the grounds of the abbey can still be used for services; today is one. As our procession climbs the gentle hill of the high street, the statue of Our Lady is borne through the gateway. We follow, still praying and singing, but once we reach the lawns that stretch out around the Lonely Arch the formation breaks up. The northern couple head off towards the priests, including Brian, who have positioned themselves around the perimeter to hear confessions. I want to go and ask his absolution for any hurt I caused him as a schoolboy, but this doesn't seem the moment. The three Irish women – who I am now convinced are sisters – hurry over to a group of friends who have been keeping them a place near the main altar that stands on the sort of platform you might put up for a rock concert. The Brummie and the young lads wander off to find a place to sit on the grass.

I walk over to the foot of the ruined arch and find myself a perch on a large, square lump of its masonry that now rests in a flower bed. Shakespeare's line – in Sonnet 73 – about 'bare ruin'd choirs where late the sweet birds sang' comes to mind. Usually taken to be the dramatist's observation on the destruction of the monasteries, it would fit neatly with the remnants of Walsingham Abbey on most days. Right now, though, the bird-song is being drowned out as the procession keeps on coming in from the high street. Towards the rear, a group of teenage pilgrims, some of the women dressed in batik dresses printed with pictures of the Virgin, have given up on 'Ave Maria's and instead are singing their own harmonies – noisily accompanied by tambourines and the sort of ululating that I had last heard at Stonehenge.

All available space in front of the altar platform is filling up quickly. A middle-aged couple come over and point at some other lumps of masonry alongside mine. 'Room for two more?' the woman asks cheerily. Her accent is Scottish and she is walking with a stick. She settles down next to me while her husband goes off to find her some water. 'It took more out of me than I'd expected,' she beams. 'I must be getting old. I used to be able to do it without even noticing.'

Marie has been coming here, she tells me, for two decades. 'My daughter was brought up on New Dawn,' she says proudly. 'Ask anyone. Diana. They'll know her. She's a beautiful girl. They all loved her. Coming here was the highlight of her year.' The use of the past tense strikes an odd note. 'Is she here with you now?' I ask, looking around as if to spot her.

'No, she's in India,' Marie replies. Nothing in her tone forbids a follow-up question.

'On holiday or gap year?'

'No, she's married a Sikh.' It may be the accent, but the final word doesn't come out with any warmth. 'She was married here first in a Catholic ceremony, and then in India.'

'Did you go?' I'm assuming she will say yes and describe a colourful meeting of cultures.

'No. We concentrated on organizing the wedding here. And it would have been expensive.' Marie is now staring into the distance. 'My sister offered us £250 towards the fares. She had just won £2 million on the National Lottery.' She pauses, then adds: 'Life doesn't always work out as you want it to.' Her husband returns with a bottle of water before I can ask any more. Her face conveys that she has said too much already and doesn't want him to know she has been confiding in a stranger.

An usher hurries past and urges us to 'tuck in'. The priests are gathering on the other side of the arch, ready to make an entrance by processing through it and up to the altar. Over the public address system someone announces that the choir, now assembled on the stage, will start the Mass with the very same 'Salve Regina' that was the last thing heard here before the abbey was dissolved.

That connection with the past is tangible as the clergy come though the arch, as countless other processions must have centuries ago. The congregation, in spite of the chaos of the seating arrangements, stand still and dignified. In the silence I can hear history being rewritten. Henry VIII could not, after all, put an end to Walsingham or shape religious belief in these islands in his own image and likeness.

The principal celebrant for the Mass is a priest from Bristol. It is, he announces as he steps forward to the bank of microphones, his first time at New Dawn. The congregation break into a spontaneous round of applause. They like clapping, I am starting to realize. Already that curious mixture of tradition and modernity typical of charismatic Christianity is obvious. 'I used to find it hard', he goes on, encouraged by their welcome, 'to wave my hands around, but this week I have been to a workshop run by Maureen' – another loud cheer – 'and now I can.' He gives us a brief demonstration of his new-found skill. More applause. And laughter. I keep my arms firmly crossed and my hands clamped to my trunk.

By the time we get to the 'Gloria', the informality has taken over totally and changed the atmosphere. The choir, augmented by the band I saw rehearsing in the tent at the Slipper Chapel, have everyone else swaying about with uplifted arms. Some of the congregation raise one, others two. Some keep them still, others might even be doing the Mexican wave at a football ground. Some cup their hands, others lay them out flat, others still look like they are saluting their Lord. And there are plenty mumbling jibberish in what is, Marie explains, an outpouring of the gift of tongues. She sits next to me, hands in her lap, mostly lost in her thoughts.

The reading is from the Book of the Apocalypse, the final bloody instalment of the New Testament. The party feel is immediately changed (presumably by design) with this account of a cosmic battle between good and evil. It all gets very solemn as the Gospel is read in English, Polish and at least two more Eastern European languages I cannot immediately identify. The story it tells is familiar – that of the Visitation, the Virgin Mary's pilgrimage across Palestine to see her aged cousin, Elizabeth, thought barren but now pregnant thanks to God's intervention.

Most biblical scholars would doubt the literal truth of this story, not least because it is told only in Luke's Gospel, but the preacher in his sermon is having nothing to do with liberal clap-trap about symbolic interpretations. This account is truth, he insists, because everything is possible when the Spirit is with you. He makes the Spirit sound like a wandering magician, dropping into every community to work miracles.

I am, I realize, alone in my reservations. The congregation is lapping it up with a hunger for truth, for certainty, for absolutes, for answers, that transforms his words into a kind of balm.

I leave just as the choir is firing up proceedings once more. As I head down the high street to the Slipper Chapel to collect my car, unable to face the jubilant post-Mass picnic in the abbey grounds, I find a part of myself already missing the companionship of the rosary procession. But that companionship comes, I reflect, at a cost. New Dawn is a package and you have to sign up for the lot. Indeed, the very act of affirming publicly and emotionally is central to getting the shot in the arm it provides. If everyone reaffirms their faith, praises the Spirit in every other sentence, sings joyfully, prays fervently and smiles at a world that otherwise would appear puzzling and even hostile, all those questions, doubts and dilemmas that are part of life away from Walsingham will fade away. Miraculously. But once you begin the homeward journey . . .

✻   ✻   ✻

A week later the thought is still troubling me. What I need to do, I decide, is disentangle Walsingham from its visitors. Or, more precisely, disentangle the continuing succour afforded by Walsingham as a sacred place from the particular agenda of New Dawn – or any other group which briefly takes up resi-

dence there. So, on a warm 15 August, the Feast of the
Assumption, I head back. Walsingham is a Marian shrine and
this is the pre-eminent Marian date in the calendar, an
occasion when the place is surely guaranteed to be itself, rather
than as others wish to refashion it.

If England had remained Catholic, today would be, as in
Italy, Spain, Portugal and Poland, a public holiday and a
festival, the occasion when the Church celebrates the unique
status it has allotted Mary, somewhere way above the rest of
humanity but just short of God. From the fifth century
onwards, Christianity was debating the notion that Christ's
mother had been 'assumed' into heaven body *and* soul, rather
than just soul which is the best the rest of us mere mortals can
hope for. It was not, however, until 1950 that Pope Pius XII
gave the official stamp of approval to the Assumption. And he
went one step further. For the only time since 1870, when the
papacy had finally been declared infallible in certain matters of
faith and morality (again after centuries of debate), Pius XII
directed that in endorsing the Assumption he was speaking
without the possibility of error. Papal infallibility is one of the
obstacles that lie in the path of Catholic–Anglican dialogue and
moves towards a closer relationship that would exorcize some
of the ghosts of the Reformation. And might ease the Christian
division made so obvious in Walsingham's two shrines.

Many Anglicans would also describe Catholic veneration of
Mary as a barrier between the denominations, but the Anglo-
Catholic Anglicans, who have been coming to Walsingham in
numbers since Hope-Patten re-established a presence here
in the 1920s, have no such qualms. They still gather, albeit in
reduced numbers in recent years, in honour of Christ's mother
at the north end of Little Walsingham in a complex of ancient
and modern buildings. In the 1930s, Hope-Patten began recre-
ating the past with the replica of the replica of the Holy House.
Then followed the Shrine Church, various chapels, accommo-
dation blocks fashioned from medieval houses, meeting rooms
and even a refectory.

It is mid-morning in the garden that joins all these different
parts of the Anglican shrine. The look, I decide, as I walk in

through an archway off Common Place, Walsingham's miniature equivalent of a central square, is that of an Oxford quad: the time-honoured buildings creating a protective shield against the outside world, the chapel in the corner, neat lawns, tastefully stocked flowerbeds and figures wandering around noiselessly, apparently in deepest concentration. The only sound comes through the open doors of the modern dining hall. Polite, clipped and largely female voices drift out and are effortlessly absorbed.

As I begin to circle round the garden by a series of interconnecting paths, however, the illusion of a college quad quickly evaporates. For a start, the grass is not flat. It contains two bumps, one featuring the three crosses of Calvary, the other topped by a tasteful pale stone outdoor altar under a white canopy stretched out on poles. I've read about them both somewhere recently. Professor Gary Waller, of the State University of New York, has written an article in *Peregrinations*, a journal for those interested in pilgrimage, claiming that Walsingham 'is today, as it must have been in the fifteenth and early sixteenth century, a place of devotion to the female religious experience – that is experience not just by, but of the female'.

It is a reasonable thesis. Most of the pilgrims scattered around the garden this morning are women. Waller starts with the figure of Mary, moves through the sale in medieval times of what was reputed to be her breast milk, and then brings his thesis bang up to date by noting Walsingham's sensual, visual approach to faith – something decidedly female, he suggests. And indeed there is certainly a softness about the setting of the Anglican shrine, though I am not convinced, on seeing the evidence first hand, by his most controversial suggestion; namely that the shrine garden contains 'a myriad reminders of the female, with all the vital parts not precisely in the recognized anatomical place, but re-arranged like a Picasso'. For Waller the two bumps are not just a landscaping device, but women's breasts. In somewhere so polite and reserved as the precincts of the Anglican shrine, it seems a curiously indecent thought.

The shrine church, opened by Hope-Patten in 1938, is long, thin and, even today, uncrowded. It contains at its heart the

Holy House, dark and slightly claustrophobic, illuminated by neat rows of candles, each with a dedication tag attached, and by the lashings of gilt on the altar. Somehow I had been expecting a table and chairs, a cot and a bed – like a real house – so am disappointed by what is in fact another very ornate chapel, as far removed from anything to be found in first-century Nazareth as can be imagined.

The church also boasts an eleventh-century well, uncovered in the 1930s when the church was being built. Medieval Walsingham had boasted two wells. The waters of each, when drunk, were reputed to have particular healing powers for those troubled by headaches and stomach aches. Finding one was, Hope-Patten believed, a mark of divine blessing, but there has been no real attempt to revive the tradition of offering cures as a rival to European Marian shrines. Walsingham – certainly at this Anglican end of town – aims rather more modestly to nurture and restore the spirit, less of a crowd-puller, it seems, but also more English and pragmatic, though pragmatism is perhaps not the first quality you associate with a Marian shrine.

It is 11.30 and pilgrims are starting to gather in the church. The decimation in Anglo-Catholic ranks caused by the Church of England's decision to ordain women priests (there will be none on the altar here today) and by the subsequent defection to Rome of many of this wing of the Church of England, has exacted its toll. There are empty seats – as if symbolizing those who have taken the papal shilling. If I want 'real' numbers here in Walsingham, I've been told, I need to head down to the Slipper Chapel.

The tent village of New Dawn has disappeared from the field opposite – to be replaced by a caravan site. Trucks, cars, vans and washing-lines are dotted around where the marquee had stood. The Travellers are one group at the Slipper Chapel today, but there is another set of pilgrims present too. As I find a slot in the car park, there are ranks of highly polished coaches with addresses in Wigan, Warrington and Preston inscribed in flowing letters on their sides. One, belonging to a firm called Eddie Brown, offers no hint of point of departure on its coachwork, instead boasting a large sign in the front window – 'On Pilgrimage'.

Inside the compound, there is the starkest of architectural contrasts to what Hope-Patten and his followers achieved at the other end of Walsingham. The Slipper Chapel aside, the Catholic shrine can hardly be described as a gem. The main Chapel of Reconciliation, the café, the bookshop and the offices are all variations on the theme of the sort of dull 1980s red-brick boxes that you might see on an out-of-town industrial estate. There is a kind of drama to the central garden, dominated by the 14 large oak crosses of the Stations of the Cross, another traditional Catholic devotion, retracing Jesus's last journey to Calvary, but the real drama here today is human. The two groups of visitors – Lancastrians and Travellers – are carefully edging round each other and their prejudices. The solid citizens of north-west England, in sensible clothes of muted colours and ample material, are eyeing the more flamboyantly dressed Traveller mothers and daughters, all elaborate manes of hair, gold hoop earrings and micro skirts.

No one can quite explain the particular connection between the faithful of Lancashire and Walsingham – though most people I ask during the course of the afternoon take a certain pride in their county being the part of the England where the changes of the Reformation were resisted most tenaciously. And equally I can find no one to give me chapter and verse on when or why 15 August at Walsingham became an annual gathering for Traveller families, most of them (like the Lancastrians) with roots in Catholic Ireland. They are clearer, though, on their reasons for coming. August 15th in Walsingham is a time for arranging marriages. Hence the elaborate clothing and almost constant parading by groups of young women.

Under the bright midday sun, people are starting to take their seats for Mass in the courtyard and, beyond, in the Chapel of Reconciliation, where a wall of glass doors has been folded back to join the indoor church with the outdoor one, on either side of the central altar. Preferring shade, I walk into the chapel, where a team of efficient ushers in blue vestments is guiding the congregation into pews. Resisting their efforts are groups of Travellers intent on a *passagiato* around the church itself, stopping occasionally to lay flowers, still wrapped in petrol station forecourt plastic, at the base of the many statues of the Virgin.

The eight priests who join forces to concelebrate the Mass are at pains throughout to join the two component parts of their congregation. They are not helped in their earnest endeavours by poor acoustics and the scarcity of natural light in the gloomy chapel. The ushers for their part try to maintain a kind of order as everyone moves forward for Communion, but the Travellers prefer a more informal route to the altar. So teeth are gritted, tolerance is stretched and tempers fray. It doesn't feel much like a celebration – of Mary, or of Walsingham.

As the Mass ends and picnics are unpacked and caravans reclaimed, I head off in search of something more sustaining in the Slipper Chapel itself. It is, surprisingly given the crowds outside, all but empty. Just two other people are kneeling in silent prayer. The inside is tiny, with pews for no more than 20. When it was built in the fourteenth century, the chapel was dedicated to Saint Catherine of Alexandria, martyred on a wheel, a death remembered today only in the spinning, sparking firework named after her. In the context of medieval Walsingham, though, she had been honoured because she was patron of pilgrims to the Holy Land.

From the outside, the chapel's antiquity is obvious, especially given the blandness of the modern buildings that surround it. Purists might argue that the early-twentieth-century exterior repair work was a little over-zealous but, once inside, they would weep in frustration. It looks and feels like an elaborate Victorian chapel of rest. There is scarcely a nod at its medieval past.

In fairness, when the neglected structure was rescued by the pious Miss Pearson Boyd, nothing would have remained of its original decorations. But other abandoned, pre-Reformation sites – such as the medieval London chapel of the bishops of Ely, now, as Saint Etheldreda's, a Catholic church near Smithfield – have been sensitively restored and brought back to life in a way that makes tangible that connection with the past. Here, even the stained glass above the altar unmistakeably

The Chapel of the Holy Spirit, next to the ancient Slipper Chapel,
at Walsingham.

belongs, in style and colour, to the mid-twentieth century. It
was designed by Geoffrey Webb specifically to celebrate
(justify, I can't help thinking as I kneel to pray) the promulga-
tion of the doctrine of the Assumption. The statue of Our Lady
of Walsingham – a replica of the medieval one which was
taken to London and burnt as an 'idol' when the abbey was
destroyed – likewise looks far too new and shiny, despite its
efforts to be true to the original. It was re-created from an
image on a surviving wax seal of Walsingham Abbey.

The history of the place, the bare footsteps of past pilgrims
who would walk without shoes into Walsingham from the
Slipper Chapel (where they cast off their slippers), is utterly
eluding me. I go with little expectation along the short
corridor that joins the Slipper Chapel to the Chapel of the
Holy Spirit. This was added in 1938 – the year the shrine was
reconsecrated by the local Catholic bishop – and so makes no
claim at all to antiquity. Inside, though, it radiates heat. The

source are the banks of lighted candles placed here day in, day out, by visitors who wish to remember and commend to God, through Mary's intercession, the sick, the dying and the dead. It is their collective flames that are lifting the temperature.

I stoop to take three new candles from a box at the back of the chapel, putting my coins in the slot (and thinking only for a fleeting second of Erasmus and his concerns about 'trade' in Falsingham). One candle for my mother, one for my father, one for my mother-in-law, all dead and sorely missed. I move forward silently in the blackened chapel to find a ledge for them. Once they are alight, I stand before them and pray silently. If the prayerful hum of the rosary procession at New Dawn hadn't quite managed ever to still my thoughts, these three flames, amid so many others, do.

One of the hardest aspects of grief is that feeling of being so powerless in the face of death. Raised in a world that celebrates, even lionizes humanity's ability to make things happen, to change, correct or cure what we don't like or want, even within ourselves, we are brought up short by the death of loved ones and reminded quite how impotent we are. It may be a tiny, futile gesture, but lighting a candle for them, and placing it in among the candles of so many others, is a comforting act of solidarity. I am not alone in mourning or in struggling to find an explanation, and they are not alone in death. As a ritual, it offers none of the answers so readily available at New Dawn, but it effortlessly gets to the core of the questions that underpin religion – questions of life, suffering and death that have no straightforward answers. In this Chapel of the Spirit, that word – Spirit – so often heard at Walsingham but so seldom defined – finally acquires a weight.

5

Holywell

As sure as what is most sure, sure as that spring
primroses shall new-dapple next year, sure as tomorrow
morning, amongst come-back-again things, things with
a revival, things with a recovery,
Thy name Winefride will live.

'Saint Winefride's Well'
by Gerard Manley Hopkins (1844–89)

The Jesuit priest-poet, Gerard Manley Hopkins, planned to write a whole verse drama about the story of Saint Winefride, but only fragments of the project remain. He was beguiled by the legend of this pious teenager, who had in AD 660 resisted so resolutely the unwanted advances of a suitor that he cut off her head, but who was then brought back to life by her saintly uncle, Beuno. Hopkins's fellow Jesuits were for almost 300 years custodians of the shrine at Holywell that marked the spot where Winefride was resurrected, 'only showing', according to her legend, 'a slender scar running round the neck'. A spring was said to have appeared at the spot where her severed head fell to earth, flowing ever since with healing waters that have been drawing pilgrims to this part of north Wales since the Middle Ages.

Hopkins's prophecy of a revival of interest in the saint's story has proved remarkably accurate. Winefride's Well boasts the longest uninterrupted history of pilgrimage of any shrine in Britain, somehow managing to escape all restrictions on Catholic activity after the Reformation. Yet by the middle decades of the nineteenth century, when Hopkins was writing, it could hardly be described as busy. However, by 1896, under an energetic

Jesuit custodian, Father Charles Beauclerk, Holywell was experiencing a spectacular boom. In the summer months there were street processions through the town by visiting Catholics carrying banners. A pilgrims' hostel was opened and numbers grew so large – 95,895 visitors painstakingly counted in Beauclerk's meticulous records for the year, with 29,000 in the month of August alone, and 2,770 bottles of its healing water despatched from the local post office – that Holywell received the ultimate Victorian accolade, the construction of its own branch line, off the main Chester to Holyhead railway, to service Saint Winefride's Halt.

That is now long closed and, at first glance, there is little in Winefride's story, or the tales of miracles associated with her well, to appeal to the sceptical and secular twenty-first century. The combination of a female Lazarus, resurrected by the healing hands of a holy man, and a site renowned down the centuries in the popular imagination for curing those the medical establishment had written off, is precisely the sort of Christianity that the scientific consensus of our age ridicules as mindless superstition or worse. 'Alleged miracles', writes the anti-religion cheerleader, Professor Richard Dawkins, in his best-selling book *The God Delusion*, 'violate the principles of science. I imagine the whole business is an embarrassment to more sophisticated circles within the Church. Why any circles worthy of the name of sophisticated remain within the Church is a mystery.'

And, if that were not enough to relegate the well to the status of a monument to the folly of credulity in ages less sophisticated than our own, then the implicit message of Winefride's tale, namely that it is better dead than raped (also promoted by the Catholic Church in the more recent story of Saint Maria Goretti), flies in the face of all modern and humane attitudes to the victims of sexual assault.

So the real miracle would appear to be that an estimated 30,000 pilgrims a year still come to Winefride's shrine, making it the most visited holy well in Britain. And, the custodians report, the numbers are rising.

*   *   *

The clouds are lined up like great bruises across the autumn sky as I near the outskirts of Holywell. Once this north-east corner of Wales, tucked beside the wide, marshy estuary of the River Dee and the English border, was a powerhouse of the industrial revolution, with mines sending out their produce via a series of small ports, but that is now only a memory. On the coast road, rusting shells of ships slowly rot, scars on a hilly landscape that, while not as spectacular as the mountain ranges further west towards Snowdonia, would otherwise have a gentle, green, billowing beauty.

Holywell used to make its living servicing local industry and providing hospitality to travellers on the long trek along the north Wales coastal corridor, but today even the main road bypasses it. And so it has reverted to what was always its main claim to fame – the well that gives the town its name. 'The Lourdes of Wales' reads a sign that marks the town boundary. 'One of the Seven Wonders of Wales' announces the notice-board at the entrance to Winefride's shrine itself.

The identity of the other six wonders briefly intrigues that trainspotter part of me that only surfaces at charity quiz nights. I've got as far as Snowdonia, Dylan Thomas and Lloyd George when the strange geography of the wooded glen rising up in front of me is sufficient to banish all other thoughts. This place was, legend tells, once devoid of water and known as Sechnant, or the 'dry valley'. Now it is awash with it and lush vegetation around buildings which, it appears, are arranged vertically rather than horizontally. Over the centuries, the shrine has developed as a series of ascending steps, piled one on top of the other, like one of those early depictions of the Last Judgement, completed before artists made use of perspective.

At the base of the canvas is the visitor centre, modern but discreet, a functional footnote and a way into the well's gardens, themselves small, neat and similarly anonymous, laid out comparatively recently on the site of an abandoned Victorian brewery which was, like much else in Holywell, named after the no doubt teetotal Winefride. After her uncle raised her from the dead, she spent her remaining fifteen years in the nearby convent of Gwytherin in Denbighshire, run by her great-aunt, whom she eventually succeeded as abbess.

One visual step up comes the arcade of three unglazed arches behind which shelters the well itself. They are built of the local reddish sandstone, which has, especially on a gloomy October day like today, a tendency to dapple into grimey blackness, offset by patches of pinky orange. The central of the three arches protrudes slightly and is the largest, flanked by smaller openings on either side. These in turn divide up at the bottom into in-and-out entrances to the well chamber, again with no doors. Taking the waters here is not for the faint-hearted.

The central arch plunges straight down into a neat rectangle of water, which stretches back from it towards the gardens. This completely open-to-the-elements outer pool, fed by the same spring, is where pilgrims finish off after, as Holywell tradition demands, bathing three times in the well itself – a custom based in Beuno's promise to Winefride that 'whoever shall at any time in whatsoever sorrow or suffering implore your aid for deliverance from sickness or misfortune, shall at the first or the second or certainly the third petition obtain his wish and rejoice at the obtainment of what he asked for'.

It wasn't until the thirteenth century, though, that these words were first reported, a gap of 500 years. The real explanation of the enduring practice may owe more to the Celtic tradition of baptism by triple immersion. Another legend – that the stone which hovers just below the surface of this outer pool is the rock where Beuno prayed, half immersed – may also have its roots in the penchant among tough, self-flagellating Celtic monks for standing in cold water to punish their bodies and so bring their souls closer to God.

Up another step in this architectural jigsaw are the two largely irrelevant (for the purposes of our story) buildings that frame and slightly crowd the central well complex at Holywell. To the left, perched on a steep-sided bluff and rising up in line with the top of the three arches, is the Anglican parish church of Saint James – solid, undistinguished, and

The water at Holywell where reputedly Saint Beuno once stood.

hardly even a shadow over proceedings below. And to the right, similarly elevated, but taller, thinner and altogether less distracting, is the former Custodian's Cottage, now the archive for Winefride's Well.

The extraordinary tableau is completed in the top of the canvas by the early-sixteenth-century well chapel, which literally sits on top of the well chamber. Its three side-windows rise up from the three arches below. The chapel has been ingeniously constructed on what are effectively stilts, presumably to accommodate the peculiar geography of this steep hillside and the rush of holy water down it towards the sea, via the Dee Estuary. As a structure, it is both a one-off and a curious combination of fragility and militancy, defying the elements but, apparently, only just. One great torrent, the sort of flash-flood that we are coming to know with other effects of climate change, and you can imagine the whole place being swept away.

My immediate impulse is to investigate the well itself that lies hidden in the gloom behind the arches. As I approach through the garden, a solitary figure is removing leaves and other debris from the outer pool with a fishing net. Hopkins described the waters here to his friend, the poet Robert Bridges, as 'clear as glass, greenish like beryl or aquamarine'. Perhaps the sun was out when he wrote that description because today they are murky and, at best, an unpoetic beige – though there may be a technical reason for this. In January 1917, mining in the Halkyn Hills behind Holywell managed to divert the underground source that fed Winefride's Well and calamitously caused it to dry up entirely. Some took it as a sign of God's disfavour at a time of war, but by September an alternative source had been located and plumbed in, and the waters began to flow again, albeit less forcefully, though apparently possessing the same miraculous powers.

In dramatic contrast to the plain colours around them are the four changing-huts, tucked into a recess behind the steps up to the Custodian's Cottage and so not visible from my original vantage point. They are flamboyant plastic-sheeted structures in blue and yellow, with pointy roofs, a modern variation on the sort of Victorian bathing-huts out of which you imagine a moustachioed man in a stripey all-over bathing suit emerging.

In the summer months there is a steady trickle of bathers in the well. Even out of season, two or three brave the cold daily. Right now, the huts are empty and zipped closed. As the pool man departs with his morning's catch, I spot a small family group gathered inside the well chamber, visible through the arches. For a public place of healing, Holywell is remarkably uncluttered. No attendants or guides or information stands crowd visitors. There are no queues, no sense of being on a production line, however holy, as you take the waters, and none of the health and safety paraphernalia associated with public access to water. People are left to their own devices, largely unsupervised, though a small red notice does ask that no one goes into the well or outer pool without first alerting the custodian at the visitor centre.

It is the father that I see first – tall, young but balding, his fluorescent orange anorak immediately visible in the shadowy recesses of the well chamber. Then a young girl of eight or nine, in a pointy lime-green winter fleece hat, dances in and out of the entrance arch. She doesn't seem to notice me. I stay back, respecting the Holywell way of doing things, but am unable entirely to look away. As my eyes discreetly search, from a distance, inside the well chamber, they finally light on a woman, seated awkwardly in a modern electric scooter-style wheelchair. Her blond head bobs in and out of view. It takes me a moment to realize that she is reaching her hand down into the water of the well, bringing herself back up straight, and then crossing herself.

My mother was a wheelchair user. I can measure out my childhood not by birthday presents received or schools attended or holidays, like most kids, but by the progressive decline in her ability to walk thanks to multiple sclerosis. First she used one stick and staggered a bit until I was seven or eight, often resting her free hand on my shoulder. Then two sticks until I was 10 or 11, falling more and more often. Briefly a zimmer frame that was clumsy and dangerous, and finally, by the time I was 12, a wheelchair. Devout in her Catholicism, she used to wonder out loud if she should make the effort to go to Lourdes, the miracle shrine in the south of France where in 1858 a young girl, Bernadette Soubirous, is said to have seen visions of the Virgin Mary. It was, in one practical way, a big ask, since she had never been abroad and never possessed a passport, but it was something else that worried her about the prospect of such a trip. 'I think I must lack the faith to be cured,' she would say, 'but I don't want to get my hopes up. Surely it's better to get used to living with something, rather than hope it will go away?'

Her intonation always suggested this was a question, but her mind was made up. She never went to Lourdes. And it wasn't just the inconvenience of the journey that prevented her because we never even came to Holywell, though I grew up only three-quarters of an hour away, on the Wirral Peninsula, on the other side of the Dee Estuary. I must have known that Holywell existed because, aged ten, I caused no end of fuss at my Catholic primary by announcing that I wanted Winefride for my confirmation saint. Boys for boys and girls for girls, I was told. I'd like to think I was being far-sighted in challenging gender stereotypes at an early age, but the truth is that I was just an awkward little boy and probably wanted to draw attention to myself.

All this is running through my mind as I watch the girl clambering onto the back of the wheelchair, anchoring it as her mother leans forward again towards the water. This is a family's simple act of faith: just to come, plunge a hand in the water, and pray. The prospect of a miracle cure is, of course, present. How can it not be in a place like this with a long history of claims of such direct interventions from God? But it is hope, and a scarcely imaginable one at that, rather than expectation. What most believers seek from such shrines is something much more earth-bound – spiritual strength and sustenance in an ongoing struggle. That, at least, is the message this family gives out as they huddle together, arms wrapped around each other.

I stand apart and search my mind for an analogy for Christian attitudes to miracle cures. Buying a lottery ticket? You don't expect to hit the jackpot, but a minor prize would be encouraging? No, it doesn't cover it. Nothing does. As an example of flying in the face of reason, knowing exactly that is what you are doing, yet still emerging from the experience (most of the time) better off, it is without parallel.

The family is making ready to leave. This is not a time for spectators, though I can't help but wonder if my mother was wrong, if there might have been something to be gained by making the short journey here. I perch on a bench in the well-garden as they emerge from the chamber. They loiter a while next to the outer pool. The father points out Beuno's stone. And embraces his wife again. As she scoots past me in her chair, I see that she is young, in her late twenties, no more, and that there are the marks of tears on her cheek. Whether of consolation and renewed courage, or of despair, I cannot tell – and will not ask.

*   *   *

I get up and start to make my way towards the now empty well chamber, but once again am sidetracked. Outside the tall, black railings that surround the compound, I spot something extraordinary. A line of curiously dressed pilgrims is making its way up the steep road that runs alongside the shrine and leads to the main entrance of the ancient chapel that hovers above the well. Dressed in long, black cassocks that button down the front from the throat to the ankle, these three elderly men sport large, gold crosses around their necks, and toad-stool-shaped black felt hats on their heads. Sprouting out from underneath are long beards and, behind, manes of grey hair. One has it tied back in a ponytail. Each is carrying a suitcase. They are, I realize, the Orthodox priests who are today bringing a taste of Eastern Christianity to this shrine in their annual Pan-Orthodox Pilgrimage. The well chamber, I decide, will have to wait. I need to see what is happening in the chapel.

Hurrying up the steep slope to the chapel entrance, I come across a group of women pilgrims. Elizabeth, in her thirties and insulated against the autumn cold by a large fur coat, has travelled up from Reading. She has a wide face and a warm smile as she turns to greet me. She talks easily and openly about her new-found allegiance to Orthodoxy. It has come, she says, at the end of a long spiritual journey. 'I was brought up and confirmed as a Catholic,' she recalls, 'but somehow I never felt at home. I was always looking for something else. I got involved in Evangelical Christianity and at one stage undertook a 40-day fast. And then one day I was in London and wandered into the Orthodox cathedral there. And it was immediate. I had come home. I think my reaction was that of many people when they find Orthodoxy. I couldn't help wondering, "Why didn't someone tell me before?"'

Alongside her, Marina and Dwynwyn are nodding in recognition. They are older and more optimistic about the weather in their colourful thin tops and anoraks. Both hail, they explain, from the Orthodox parish of Saint Aidan's in Levenshulme in south-east Manchester. 'We started out about 15 years ago with just 20 of us in a borrowed room in Stockport,' Marina tells me, 'and now we are 80 in our own church. We come here every year on the pilgrimage.'

Both women were originally churchgoing Anglicans. Marina first felt drawn to Orthodoxy when she went on a pilgrimage to Jerusalem in the late 1980s. 'It was the first time I had ever been in an Orthodox church and, like Elizabeth, I immediately felt it was where I was meant to be.' There were, she admits, more practical issues that also played a part in her decision to convert. 'I date it back to that Bishop of Durham,' she says of her disaffection with the Church of England. On his appointment in 1984, David Jenkins caused controversy by publicly doubting the physical reality of the resurrection of Jesus, a key tenet of the Christian faith for many. Jenkins's views were not so unusual in the academic theological circles where he had moved before being named as Bishop of Durham, but scandalized many Anglican churchgoers. They were only confirmed in their doubts about him when a bolt of lightning caused extensive damage at York Minister three days after his consecration. 'I felt there was so much dispute and disagreement in the Church of England,' remembers Dwynwyn. 'Whereas here it is all peace. We have no arguments because the Orthodox have never changed the way we do things.'

Orthodox Christians gather in Holywell's well chamber.

The annual publication of churchgoing statistics in Britain is usually an occasion for hand-wringing among Anglicans, Catholics and Non-Conformists alike. Year on year, attendances continue to drop, even though around 70 per cent of

British people still call themselves Christian. They are evidently drawn to the idea but not the institutions that claim to enshrine it. There was a reported decline of half a million in churchgoers between 1998 and 2005, and only two growth areas in the general picture of doom and gloom. At one end of the spectrum, numbers of Evangelicals, often organized in small, independent, black-led churches, are rising. And at the other, there has been a marked increase in the numbers of Orthodox Christians in Britain to around 350,000.

It is, admittedly, from a small base, and can be partially accounted for by the influx of migrants from Eastern Europe where Orthodoxy is often the predominant form of Christianity. But there is another story behind these figures, as Elizabeth, Marina and Dwynwyn demonstrate. Significant numbers of members of other mainstream Christian churches are finding a home in Orthodoxy, driving the establishment of a new network of parishes around the country (almost 200 and rising), often in the disused premises of other denominations that can no longer attract a congregation.

That trickle towards Orthodoxy became more of a flow after the General Synod of the Church of England voted to ordain women in 1992. While many Anglicans who felt that their church did not have the authority to break with tradition and permit women priests opted to join Rome, others came over to Orthodoxy in the same period, valuing its best-known claim to represent an unchanging attitude to the faith. This is summed up rather neatly in a slogan on one of Orthodoxy's British websites which reads, 'Telling the Truth since AD 33'. 'I'm not one for women priests,' says Marina. 'It wasn't why I became Orthodox, but I'm definitely not in favour.'

We have reached the entrance to the chapel. I let the others go in first and watch as they join groups of friends. This is a kind of gathering of the Orthodox clans, mainly from around the north-west of England and north Wales. The small, almost square chapel has been cleared of pews, chairs and clutter – as is the Orthodox way. Worshippers stand, if they possibly can. Four icons – central to Orthodox worship but on the margins of the Western Christian Church since the break between East and West around 1054 – have been placed, resting on tall stands (analoys), at intervals in front of the altar. All show the Madonna and Child. Next to them, banks of lanky honey-coloured candles burn in trays of sand. In an Orthodox church, there would be a screen – or iconostasis – between the altar and the congregation, but here the pilgrims are making do and mend in borrowed premises.

At a side table, the priests who had earlier been walking up the hill are now changing into the ornate, colourful vestments they take out of their suitcases. There is already a heady smell of rose incense. I find myself a quiet corner in the chapel where once pilgrims would pray and hold an all-night vigil before bathing in the well below. I quickly tally up a congregation of around 100, with a wide variety of ages. Divine Liturgy – the Eucharistic service in Orthodoxy – is about to begin. While we wait, a single female voice is reading from the Bible in a rhythmic chant, bringing a stillness amid the bustle of preparation that persists, even when she momentarily breaks off to clear her throat.

The chapel dates back to Holywell's immediate pre-Reformation heyday. Henry V made a pilgrimage here to thank Winefride for her part in his victory at Agincourt in 1415. Edward IV and Richard III both subsequently paid public homage to the saint of Holywell. And it was Lady Margaret Beaufort, mother of Henry VII, who is thought to have been among the principal funders of the construction of the present chapel and its well chamber crypt below. No one is entirely sure what was here before by way of shelter for pilgrims to the well, but in 1427, the papal registers report, Pope Martin V allowed a grant of indulgences for those giving alms to repair of 'the chapel of Holliwell' because the building had collapsed. So there was something.

Unlike the well chamber, which has never ceased to be used for its original purpose, the chapel has played many roles since the Reformation. It has been variously a courthouse and a school and, as a result, has suffered damage to its layout, decoration and design that could only partially be put right when it was restored in 1976. The direct link from chapel to crypt and its well has gone. You have to walk round along the street. Even the ownership is now split. The local Catholic diocese runs the well and a secular conservation body owns the chapel – though the two are part of the same structure. Regular Anglican worship is in the parish church next door, while Holywell's Catholic parish meets further up the hill in a former inn, rebuilt as a church in the first half of the nineteenth century.

Whatever its sufferings down the ages – and the ugly concrete floor is the worst scar on an otherwise still dignified building – the chapel maintains an aura. Perhaps it is the chanting and the gathering of pilgrims, here today as they have been down the centuries. Or it may be the intricate but worn carvings that have survived the vandals of time on the roof and supporting timbers. They recall a lost age of magnificence – animals, angels and acorns whose significance would once have been readily recognized by worshippers, but whose origins are now obscure.

The priests are making their way towards the altar, five of them of varying ages and sizes. The Divine Liturgy to be celebrated is that of Saint John Chrysostom, the fourth-century Bishop of Constantinople, venerated equally in Western and Eastern halves of Christianity. That common ground in an undivided Christian Church, before the split, is also part of the Orthodox attachment to Holywell. This is their twenty-second year of coming here on pilgrimage. In the history of the place is a thread that joins them to the first pilgrims, believed to have flocked here in the eighth century to sample the healing waters. And in Winefride, the Orthodox see a saint who pre-dates the division between Rome and Constantinople and who – like John Chrysostom – represents a unifying force. As Father Gregory Hallam, the former Anglican vicar who is leading us in the Divine Liturgy, tells me later, 'Veneration of Western saints who are also part of our Orthodox patrimony is an excellent thing to do. It affirms and rejoices in the common patrimony between the Greek East and Latin West.'

Or as Marina puts it rather more bluntly of Winefride, 'She's Orthodox too.'

That a shrine to a pre-division saint exists in Wales, within striking distance of many Orthodox parishes in the region, also allows what is still for most a rather foreign, exotic brand of Christianity to reclaim roots in these islands, thus making the idea of being English *and* Orthodox seem less peculiar, though not entirely natural. Nicola, one of the pilgrims and a lawyer in her twenties from a Cypriot Orthodox family, tells me of her astonishment when she and her husband, having moved from London to Lancashire for work, discovered a newly opened Orthodox parish in Leyland, made up mainly of English converts. 'We were used to our own churches in London. And my husband is properly Greek. So when we went in, we frankly couldn't believe our eyes. Everybody was English but they were doing what we do – or sort of doing it. It was very strange – Orthodox but not Greek. But over time we have grown to like it, to fit in.' She stops and laughs, 'But it's still not the same.'

That connection which Holywell offers the English Orthodox has another dimension. When individuals convert to Orthodoxy – or, as they would put it more technically, are chrismated, a rough equivalent of confirmation, when those who have been baptized in other Christian denominations are anointed with oil of chrism and welcomed into the Orthodox fold – the usual practice is for them to take the name of a Christian saint of the first millennium. 'I was Marjorie,' explains Marina, 'but there's no Saint Marjorie for the Orthodox, so I chose Marina. The two are quite close.' And quite different too. What about her non-Orthodox friends, I ask? What do they call her now? 'Oh, Marjorie mostly.' She shrugs. Reinvention can only stretch so far.

The Orthodox liturgy does not have quite the same effect on me as it did on her, or on others gathered here. There is undeniably a time-honoured, unaltered beauty to it, free from the clumsy modernizations inflicted on Western liturgies in the name of progress or populism. The chanting of the sung responses has an immediate other-worldly quality to it, and in its repetitions and cycles of prayers, it manages somehow to capture an essence of the transcendent, or at least lift me sufficiently out of the everyday so that something transcendent might be potentially glimpsed. But it is also simultaneously achingly familiar for anybody brought up in the Western tradition of mainstream Christianity. Not radically different enough, in and of itself, to prompt a conversion, unless there were other reasons too.

The great prayers are, of course, shared in common between both branches of the Christian family, though here the 'Our Father' is repeated after the English version in Romanian, Greek and another Slav language I don't recognize, to acknowledge the presence, among the ranks of the English converts, of cradle Orthodox from other parts of Europe. The split in the chapel is, I estimate as I watch the lips of those who join in the variations of the prayer, about 60–40 in favour of the home-grown converts.

The first big difference in liturgy between East and West I discern is in my legs. No pews is a challenge, though not entirely unknown when I turn up in my own church too late and have to stand because there are no seats. There, however, the physical strain is all done-and-dusted in, at the very most, an hour. 'Father does a good quick Mass,' my Irish Catholic mother-in-law used to say, by way of recommendation. Here, we are still going strong after an hour and three-quarters. 'You get used to it,' Dwynwyn (née Jean) reassures me later. 'It's good for your leg muscles,' agrees Elizabeth (née Beverley).

The arms also get their fair share of exercise as there is much crossing yourself and bending with one hand – thumb, index finger and middle finger bunched together to represent the Holy Trinity – to touch the ground in *metania*, an Eastern form of genuflection.

The Orthodox, Father Gregory (né Graham) points out subsequently, cross themselves in a different order from Western Christians. Shamefacedly, I admit that I hadn't noticed. 'You go from left shoulder to right shoulder,' he explains, 'we go

Orthodox priests bless Winefride's well.

from right to left.' I must be looking puzzled because he then puts me through a routine. 'Bear with me,' he says, 'there is a point to this. You face me.' I do, looking round to check that we are not making too much of a spectacle of ourselves. 'Now my daughter teaches dance, and when she does, she is always facing her pupils. So when she says to them, "You move your right", she shows them by moving her left' – he kicks his left foot – 'because she is facing them. She is their mirror image. And it is like that for us. So when I make the sign of the cross, I go from left to right' – he demonstrates – 'but the congregation copies me and goes right to left.' My hand is hovering, confused, between my shoulders. 'Somewhere along the line, though, Western Christians started doing it the same way as their priests, not as a mirror image.'

This may be a matter that has prompted centuries of theological dispute – and there are plenty of other more densely

theological arguments about the respective symbolic importance of doing it either way round – but I can't help thinking it
is precisely the sort of nicety that puts most people off organized religion. Not that Father Gregory is at all keen to emphasize denominational differences. Quite the opposite. 'I am not
interested', he says, 'in rigid demarcations. If you take the
saints, for example. It's not a case of who is in and who is out.
A lot of Orthodox would look favourably on Western saints
who came after the split between East and West such as
Thomas Aquinas and Francis of Assisi.'

Gregory was a priest in the Anglo-Catholic or 'High' wing
of the Church of England until 1995. He left, he says, not
because he opposed women priests, but over a theological
issue – his understanding of salvation. 'There is too much
emphasis in the West on original sin and the effects of original
sin. The East has more houseroom for the resurrection and so
our understanding of humanity is more optimistic, hopeful,
and shot through with the glory of God.' It's a nice phrase –
and comes, if I am not mistaken, appropriately enough from
Manley Hopkins.

What about the unchangingness of Orthodoxy, though? Did
that not have a particular appeal at a time when Father
Gregory's Anglican world was being turned upside-down by a
democratic vote by General Synod? 'We do, you are right,
have a deep awareness of our history, but we do change. I'm
not against the ordination of women in principle, but I do have
a difficulty. As an Anglican, any decision can only make sense
if you do what the rest of Christianity is doing. In essential
matters, the unity of the whole Christian Church – Catholic,
Orthodox and Anglican – must have the first call. And the
Church of England was ignoring that.'

*   *   *

At the end of Divine Liturgy, chairs reappear in the chapel for
those novices, like me, whose knees are buckling under the
endurance test of an Orthodox liturgy. The pilgrims settle

down in groups for lunch. Matthew, who had carried an icon during a short procession that was part of the service, offers me a sandwich. He's a former Anglican in his forties and runs a fair trade gift shop in Chester, though he belongs to an Orthodox parish further into Wales in the slate-mining town of Blaenau Ffestiniog. What draws him back each year on this Orthodox pilgrimage to Holywell, he explains, is the history of unbroken pilgrimage here, that sense of being part of something bigger and longer. 'In Orthodoxy, we often use the phrase "Was, is and will be", and you get that here in the ancient tradition of prayer and healing at the well.'

It is usually said that pilgrims started visiting the well in the seventh century, soon after Winefride was miraculously brought back to life. The earliest surviving evidence for a shrine here, however, comes in 1093, when the wife of one of William the Conqueror's followers gifted 'Holiwell' to some Benedictine monks in Chester. There is, though, no mention in the Domesday Book, compiled seven years earlier, so it cannot have been a place of much significance back then.

Winefride's own story can be traced back only to the twelfth century and to two written sources. The first is by the same monks of Saint Werburgh's Abbey in Chester who had been made custodians in the times of William the Conqueror. The second, slightly later and largely following the first but with embellishments, comes from the pen of Robert, Prior of Shrewsbury Abbey.

The monks tell how the young Winefride had been left at home when her noble parents went off to a service led by their relative, Beuno, at his nearby monastery, presumed to be on the site of the current well. Caradog, the son of a local chieftain, called by on his way back from hunting and, finding Winefride alone, tried to rape her. She fled in terror.

The girl had all but reached the door of the monastery where she hoped to obtain protection from God, and from Beuno, and was just about to step across the threshold, when he [Caradog] reached her with his sword and cut off her head. And on the spot where her blood had flowed there was an earthquake with a loud noise and a great stream of water burst forth and has continued to flow from that day to this . . . Rushing from the church, Beuno saw Caradog wiping his sword upon the grass and cursed him so that his body melted away and his soul was carried to hell. Beuno placed Winefride's head back on her body and prayed over her. His prayer was heard. The body returned at once to life and animation.

The distance of five centuries between the events described and this account must raise doubts about its accuracy, even among those prepared to believe that severed heads can be reconnected with bodies through God's intervention. There is a slight historical basis for thinking that a highborn Winefride did exist in the seventh century. Her brother, Owain, is mentioned in some chronicles. Yet her story is not unlike that of several others in the Christian tradition and so may be based on an archetype. One popular account, for instance, says that Saint Paul was not crucified on the orders of Emperor Nero in AD 64, but beheaded, and that his severed head bounced three times. On each spot, a fountain sprang up, immortalized to this day in the Three Fountains Abbey in Rome. Moreover, in Celtic folklore, skulls are said to have special powers, including healing. At Saint Teilo's Well at Llandeilo Llwydarth in Pembrokeshire, the waters are reputed to cure whooping cough, but only if drunk out of the remains of this sixth-century saint's skull.

And the annals of the saints contain several similar stories to Winefride's from the early Church. Saint Denys was, in the third century, beheaded on the Parisian hill that became Montmartre – 'mountain of martyrs' – but picked up his head and walked for two miles, preaching all the time, until he reached the spot where today stands the Basilica of Saint Denys, burial place of French kings. His statue is at the left portal of Notre Dame and he is, with a whimsical but aspirational grasp of medicine, the patron saint of headache sufferers. If we could all just take off our heads when they are hurting . . . Closer to home for Winefride's is the tale of Saint Lludd, which pre-dates hers by roughly 100 years. Lludd was beheaded in Brecon when resisting a man's brutal advances. Penginger Well sprang up where her head landed.

What is also intriguing is the spread of Winefride's fame, over and above all the other saints and holy wells of Wales, and into royal circles in the late Middle Ages. It is here that Prior Robert's alternative account of her life gives a clue. There is an argument which says that any cult around Winefride was local and small scale until the monks of Shrewsbury, led by their Prior, Robert, unearthed her remains from the graveyard of her former convent and put them on display in their abbey in 1138.

This was an age when any aspiring great abbey, monastery or church needed to display a saint's relics – a finger, a thumb, a leg, eyeballs, or a lock of hair – to draw the crowds. To modern sensibilities, it is ghoulish and superstitious. Medieval, in fact, in the way that we use the word now, as an alternative for ignorant or misguided. But also medieval in the truest sense of the word – pertaining to the medieval period, a time without our squeamishness, faith in science or access to doctors and medicines, when relics were seen as a route to God's favour and protection when life was very often hanging by a thread. Touching them – or their casing – or merely making the effort to come before them as a pilgrim in prayer, was believed to be enough to effect a miracle cure, or to obtain spiritual succour and support in the struggle that was life. Which carries me back to the mother in the wheelchair – mine and the one I saw earlier.

So, lacking a local saint, the monks of Shrewsbury decided to appropriate Winefride whose resting-place was no more than 50 miles away and whose modest cult had already reached their ears. And they did so very successfully. So suc-cessfully, in fact, that pilgrims also began going both to Wine-fride's original grave – where they would lie down on the earth in the hope of a cure – and to Holywell itself.

There were several layers to this devotion. Many relics or holy wells were associated with male saints or martyrs. Winefride, by contrast, was particularly popular with women – and Holywell had a reputation for curing what my father would have called 'women's problems'. For Lady Margaret Beaufort, the appeal of Winefride's cult may have been reinforced by their shared association with Wales. Though born in England, Margaret had either given birth to her son, the future Henry VII, in Pembroke Castle, or raised him there after his father's death. Her father-in-law was Welsh, and when her son began his challenge for the English throne, supported vigorously by his mother, he did so with strong Welsh backing. For Margaret to be so public in her devotion to a Welsh saint may then have also had a political dimension – to be seen to be Welsh – as well as a private one. (Once King, Henry commissioned a statue of Winefride for his chapel in Westminster Abbey.)

By the early fifteenth century, Winefride's feast day – 22 June – had become a major solemnity throughout Wales *and* England, but when Margaret Beaufort's grandson, Henry VIII, ordered the Dissolution of the Monasteries in 1537, both Shrewsbury Abbey and Basingwerk, the local abbey to Holywell, were destroyed and Winefride's relics scattered. Yet in the wholesale destruction of church property of the English Reformation and the centuries of persecution of Catholics that followed, the well itself seems to have survived remarkably unscarred. And even more remarkably, Catholic pilgrims continued to come to what the new national Church regarded as an illegal place of worship.

We know about these visits by the Recusant Catholics from the various unsuccessful attempts to stop them. In 1579, Queen Elizabeth's Council of the Marches hatched a plan to poison the water at Holywell to put an end to the practice, but it clearly didn't work because by 1625 the Anglican Bishop of Bangor in north Wales was complaining to the House of Lords that 'there is a great concourse of people at St Winefride's Well and public mass is said continually'.

Quite why the well got away with it when every other public display of Catholicism was stamped out and driven into hiding is hard to know. The persecution of the Recusants, from the reign of Elizabeth through to the late eighteenth century, and finally the Catholic Emancipation Act of 1829, is well recorded. Where the Catholic faith remained strong, it did so in secret, in the priest-holes and disguised chapels of Recusant stately homes such as Stonor Park in Oxfordshire or Oxburgh Hall in Norfolk. At Holywell, with its open-sided crypt, there was no way of hiding – and apparently little attempt to do so.

One explanation is that local townspeople and justices of the peace had too much respect for the well – and too much to gain from its continuing to bring people to Holywell – to close it down, but the pilgrimage trade must have been a shadow of its former self. Another thought is that people bathing in the waters was not quite the same as attending a prohibited Catholic Mass. For that, in the times of persecution, you had to go to secret rooms at two Holywell inns, the Cross Keys and the Star.

Only briefly, during the short reign of James II, from 1685 to 1689, did Catholicism come out into the open again in Holywell with a great flourish, as Britain's last Catholic monarch visited the shrine with his wife, Mary of Modena, to pray for a son. He bequeathed to it a relic of his Stuart ancestor, Mary Queen of Scots, the Catholic pretender to Elizabeth's throne, executed by her cousin in 1587.

And Holywell didn't escape the persecution entirely. As early as 1582 its resident priest, Father John Bennet, was captured and put on trial for treason. The court had to meet in the chapel above the well because of an epidemic raging in the surrounding county. Bennet was sentenced to death, but later it was commuted to banishment. In 1637, vandals disfigured the fabric of the well, while in 1656, Father Humphry Evans, head of what had by now become an illegal Jesuit mission around the well, was arrested and beaten. Fourteen years later, one of his successors, Father John Plessington, was caught up in the wave of anti-Catholic hysteria that surrounded the alleged Titus Oates Plot to unseat the King and replace him with a Catholic, and was executed at nearby Chester.

But the story that most catches my imagination from this period is that of Edward Oldcorne, another Jesuit priest, who was part of the network of secret Catholic Mass centres in Worcestershire. On 3 November 1601, he came on pilgrimage to Holywell and bathed in its waters, and was cured of what is variously described as gangrene on the roof of his mouth, or cancer of the throat. Before he became a priest, Oldcorne had been a doctor. Did he struggle to reconcile his two vocations over his 'cure'? The gulf between the two would not have been so great in the early seventeenth century as it is today, but large enough to have caused him to think.

Presumably not for too long, though, for in 1605 he returned to give thanks to Saint Winefride for saving his life. He brought with him a group of fellow Recusants that included Everard Digby, later that year exposed as one of the key plotters, along with Guy Fawkes, in plans to blow up Parliament on 5 November. Oldcorne's guilt came by association. Even under torture in the Tower of London, he did not incriminate himself.

On 7 April 1606, in Worcester, he was half hanged until he began to pass out, cut down and disembowelled while still alive, then castrated, and finally his heart was removed. His body was decapitated, cut into quarters and then parboiled before being displayed at prominent sites around the city. One of his eyeballs was forced out of its socket by the impact of the axe's blow, and was scooped up by a pious onlooker. It became another relic, treasured by Recusant Catholics, and remains in the possession of the Jesuits of Stonyhurst.

Oldcorne's 'miracle cure' had gained him five years and arguably a more gruesome death, but the name of Winefride was said to have been on his lips as the axe fell.

*　　　*　　　*

The procession down to the well is beginning to filter out of the chapel entrance. At its head are the five Orthodox priests, one carrying a reliquary – a framed glass container on a gold-encrusted pole, usually in the safe keeping of the local Catholic priest, but on loan today in a commendable ecumenical gesture to the Orthodox. It contains a tiny fragment of Winefride's relics, apparently saved when Shrewsbury Abbey was dissolved in 1537, sent to Rome for safe keeping, and returned, as a mark of official favour for Holywell, in the nineteenth century. Quite which bit of Winefride it is – if anything at all – is impossible to tell. It is like no part of a human body I have ever seen, literally a fragment of dark, hard material. In contrast to those medieval pilgrims whose greatest hope would have been to brush against the saint's relics, today's visitors seem to regard the elaborate casing of the reliquary as a warning that its fabled contents are made of the most fragile china and so could be damaged irrevocably if anyone so much as looked at them for more than a split second.

The five priests are surrounded by members of the congregation bearing icons and, in one case, an incense burner whose bells ring out as he swings it. The townspeople of Holywell, driving past on the way up to the local branch of Aldi, hardly spare us a glance. They must have become so accustomed to such sights on a road they call Well Street – Upper and Lower.

We re-enter the well gardens through gates that have been specially opened for the occasion. As we walk, Rosemary, a woman in her sixties in a headscarf, tells me how she joined the Orthodox after rejecting Catholicism following the changes brought in by the reforming Second Vatican Council of the 1960s. Which changes in particular? I wonder politely. 'Oh, I can't remember now,' she smiles. She was briefly an Anglican, but left, she recalls, as soon as talk began over women priests.

The square well chamber is simply breathtaking. Part of its élan is its obvious state of decay. Stone carvings are so worn as to be unrecognizable, and the graffiti, scratched onto its walls by pilgrims down the ages, puts me in mind of a bus shelter

that has been targeted by vandals. Only this is the most sump-
tuous bus shelter I've ever been in. And the graffiti is also definitely superior. The elaborate *Khi Ro* – the Greek letters
standing for Christ – can just about be discerned in one spot,
accompanied by the date 1627.

I don't need to be told the chamber is ancient. I can see it
with my own eyes. It has suffered no clumsy though well-
intentioned restoration such as that undertaken at Walsingham's Slipper Chapel. Last year, Rosemary confides, they
weren't able to come inside at all because it was judged unsafe.
Bits of stonework had fallen from the ceiling and it was feared
others might follow. I glance up nervously as we process round
the well itself, but it all looks pretty secure.

The three outer walls of the chamber, joined at the front by
the arcade of three arches, are holding back the hillside. Each
is blackened by centuries of smoke from the candles of the
faithful that surround a large statue of Saint Winefride, a nineteenth-century copy of the original destroyed in the Reformation, but with that thin line around her neck plainly visible.
Once, another pilgrim tells me, this backdrop would have been
blue and red and gold. 'We would all get a shock if we saw
how colourful the medieval church really was,' he says. 'They
didn't do solemn.'

In the centre is the well itself. Its waist-high surrounding
walls are arranged in a star shape, creating five recesses.
Alongside the star, and once separated by a wall that is now
only visible just below the water level, is an oblong bath.
Pilgrims climb down one set of steps so as to bathe in the
waters, and then exit via another set of steps at the other end.
Each point of the star, and the corners of the oblong bath,
bears the slender, crumbling, orange stone pillars that reach up
to the fan-vaulted ceiling. They are no thicker than a child's
leg, and it is an architectural miracle that they manage both to
support the chapel above and remain straight in the face of the
sheer momentum of the land down the hillside.

The well water itself, the palest of pale blues, is gently
bubbling up from its underground source. It is, I have been

Divine Liturgy in Winefride's chapel.

told many times today, absolutely freezing, though even on the coldest of days it doesn't ice over. Father John Gerard, a Recusant priest later implicated in the Gunpowder Plot, recorded in his journal a visit he made in November 1593. 'There was a hard frost . . . and the ice in the stream had been broken . . . But frost or no frost, I went down into the well like a good pilgrim. For a quarter of an hour, I lay down in the water and prayed. When I came out my shirt was dripping, but I kept it on and pulled all my clothes over it and was none the worse for my bathe.'

I feel ashamed of being so nesh and failing to follow his robust example on a relatively mild October day. Perhaps I have inherited a particular lack of faith in miracles from my mother. And there are, I excuse myself, too many people around. To go in the water would be ostentatious – and embarrassing.

Instead I lean over the side and peer in. The bottom is visible, about seven feet down. I can just about make out a darkish blob. Legend has it that it is the blood that Winefride's severed head left behind. Science, however, has disproved this particular tale. The moss at the bottom of the well is of a particular variety that has, on occasion, a reddish hue. The scientists have also taken samples of the water over the years to check if it contains any special ingredient or unusual balance of minerals. So far, to no avail. There is no obvious answer to why these waters have a reputation for healing. Other, that is, than the obvious answer of the faith of the bathers – and science doesn't seem that keen on measuring faith.

I recently attended a seminar on science and religion where work, published in September 2008 by academics at the Oxford Centre for Science of the Mind, was discussed. In an admittedly small-scale experiment, they had given electric shocks to 12 Catholics and 12 atheists as they studied a painting of the Virgin Mary. They found that the Catholics seemed able to block out much of the pain, apparently thanks to the painting. Using brain-scanning techniques, they discovered that the Catholics were activating part of the brain associated with conditioning the experience of pain. It might also, they tentatively suggested, be seen as a kind of religious lobe in the brain, more active in those with faith than otherwise. For me it was an intriguing thought, an example of the potential for fruitful collaboration between religion and science, but not one that excited much enthusiasm among the Oxford team's peers. They laughed it off as 'pseudo-science', 'soft science' and 'the sort of thing you do on a Friday afternoon to make headlines in newspapers'.

As the priests move on to bless the well-waters, dipping in three times a crucifix on a long rope, I start examining the ceiling. Like the pillars, it is the product of delicate and extremely intricate carving. The arches of the vaulting meet in a series of bosses. Over the well itself, the large, dangling pendant of round stone depicts scenes from the life of Winefride, only just discernible because the detail is so badly worn. Elsewhere there are coats of arms – Margaret Beaufort's, Catherine of Aragon's, and that of the Stanley family, local landowners and one-time benefactors – but in the gloom and decay it is hard to make out their exact composition. It is as if each has been soaked and disfigured by the all-pervading damp of the chamber into a series of bumps and lumps. Some vignettes can, however, still be appreciated. On the ceiling over the steps leading into the well are two pilgrim faces, one slightly in front of the other, with his arm round his companion's neck and shoulders, as if supporting him, or carrying him through the waters.

There used to be a row of crutches kept in the well chamber, discarded by cured bathers – a similar display is in the grotto at Lourdes, as I discovered on my teenage trip there – but it has been removed to the small museum in the visitor centre. Saint Winefride's Well does not shout about its reputed powers. It learnt in post-Reformation times to be discreet, and the habit has evidently been hard to break. In the age of science, it wears its reputation for healing lightly. That is its appeal.

The Orthodox pilgrims are now chanting from the ancient liturgy of Winefride. 'Through thy pious intercession, we may receive perfect health of our souls and bodies, O Holy Virgin and Martyr pray for us.' The incense is becoming slightly overpowering and I move towards the open side of the chamber for fresh air. As I do, a family are quietly kneeling by the outer pool, ignoring what is going on inside. The mother is dipping her hands in the waters and making the sign of the cross on the heads of each of her blond-haired children. The father is filling a bottle with well-water from a small tap. I have it in my mind that they are Irish on the basis of a stray remark an old friend made when I told her I was going to Holywell. 'We'd always drop in there on the way to catch the ferry to Ireland from Holyhead in Anglesey,' she remembered. 'Out of the car, to the well, cross ourselves, and then back on the road.'

It is how it has been here for centuries. Whether you come for a few minutes, like this family, or a few hours, like the Orthodox pilgrims inside the well chamber behind me, you are joining a human chain that stretches back through the centuries, containing kings and poets, the dedicated and the desperate, and which offers no other connection than a simple faith in something that, to contemporary secular ears, is literally incredible. And there is, I realize in that moment, watching the family return to their car, a great deal of comfort to be derived from being a link in that chain.

6

Iona

How sad a welcome! To each voyager
Some ragged child holds up for sale a store
Of wave-worn pebbles, pleading on the shore
Where once came monk and nun with gentle stir,
Blessings to give, news ask, or suit prefer.
Yet is yon neat trim church a grateful speck
Of novelty amid the sacred wreck
Strewn far and wide. Think, proud Philosopher!
Fallen though she be, this Glory of the west,
Still on her sons, the beams of mercy shine . . .

'Upon Landing', William Wordsworth (1833)

Iona is not for the faint-hearted pilgrim. In the jet-engine age of swift gratification, its remoteness is part of the spiritual pull of this small Hebridean island. I leave my home in London just before five in the morning and am in almost perpetual motion by train, bus and boat, even cutting the various connections fine, and still only just get there in time to witness a sunset to justify Wordsworth's claims for 'this Glory of the west'.

As the hours in transit tick by, though, I begin to suspect that the trek itself is not simply to be endured and filled by newspapers, books and phone calls. It has an importance in its own right – the getting there being, if not as important as the arriving, then certainly somewhere on the same scale. For it slows visitors down and thereby acclimatizes them to the other world they are about to encounter on Saint Columba's Isle, reputedly in AD 563 the birthplace of Scottish and, in some accounts, of British Christianity (though we must examine that claim in a minute). Cities can be rather like particle accelerators – they take people predisposed to be in a hurry and entice them to go even quicker. While, in theory, slowing down is a state of mind and so should be possible when in the metropolis with a little willpower, many of us are somehow wired only to loosen our grip on the fast lane when transported to open countryside – better still, an island. Something about the empty and spectacular landscape, the monotonous beauty of the sea, encourages us to let go. It was on 'the Lake Isle of Innisfree' that W. B. Yeats could finally find peace where 'peace comes dropping slow'.

The whole journey is, in effect, a process of winding down; unconscious at first but, once recognized, embraced. The train from busy London (even at 5 a.m.) to bustling Glasgow bowls along, fast and direct, covering 400 miles in just short of five hours, the whole operation geared to time-poor, demand-laden passengers with its wireless connections and tableside plugs for computers. Blinds on the window pull down to improve focus on laptop screen and blot out spires, mills and peaks that might be distractions from the here and now.

The second stage forces a change of gear. The West Highland Line from Glasgow to Oban covers a quarter of the distance of the first leg in two-thirds of the time. Mobile phones become redundant as we climb through signal-blocking mountains, and Blackberries and 'required reading' begin to pale next to the view out of the unblinded windows of the sturdy, spartan carriages as they skirt alongside lochs, plunge into forest tunnels and linger at well-maintained halts with teashops that could effortlessly host a *Brief Encounter* between Trevor Howard and Celia Johnson.

As the miles-per-hour counter tumbles to what feels like single digits, it suddenly seems pointless even to look at my watch. It will take as long as it takes. With that realization, I can feel a space beginning to open up inside me.

Next I find myself sitting on the upper deck of the slow, stately ferry that crosses from Oban to Mull, being washed by a landscape of velvety cliffs, lonely lighthouses and acre after acre of pure blue sea and sky. Then there is a coach, the sort of coach that used to take us on school outings in the 1970s, all hard, upright, plush nylon seats, narrow aisles and understeer, only this time minus the ashtrays in the back of the seat in front. It runs east to west across the no longer alien but increasingly intriguing emptiness of Mull from Craignure to Fionnphort ('fin-a-fort'). Runs is the wrong word. The single-track road that crosses the Ross of Mull would be better suited to tractors. So the coach takes its time and lingers long and patiently in the elaborately signposted passing-places.

As I wait on another jetty for the ferry to Iona, an elderly fisherman with the long, matted grey hair and piercing blue eyes that every children's book ascribes to a seafarer, wanders over to chat animatedly to the other two passengers, all three of them evidently locals. Phrases catch on the breeze and drift over. 'There's no stress on Iona,' he says emphatically at one juncture. 'It's only when you get over here.' The distinction he is making between Mull and Iona means nothing to me as yet, but sounds enticing. If I am unstressed now, how much further can I go?

It takes only ten minutes to cross the half-mile sound where the depths of a millpond sea are graded in differing shades of turquoise. This is reportedly a sealife playground with even the occasional sperm whale dropping in to frolic, but it is late in the day and maybe they have headed home already. Instead Iona bobs serene and alone on the near horizon, its elemental landscape of tough-looking, stumpy, stoney hills sliding down to bleached white sands apparently little changed since the Ice Age receded 20,000 years ago.

To complete the casting off of modern cares and comforts, landing is followed by the most ancient form of transport of the lot – a walk up the hill (only the 100 or so permanent residents are allowed to keep cars on the island) to Iona Abbey, originally a cluster of wood, stone and clay monks' cells when Columba made it his base in the sixth century, later until the Reformation, the squat, sturdy, stone-built Benedictine Cathedral of the Isles, subsequently a ruin, and finally, since the late 1930s, restored as the home to the internationally renowned

Iona seen from across the Sound.

ecumenical Iona Community founded by George MacLeod.

MacLeod recognized in Iona an innate sense of place. It wasn't just the slowness of life on this remote outcrop that struck him. Like many other visitors, he discovered that Iona and its people could open an otherwise hidden door into history. Iona had, he became convinced, the power to skip back centuries in the blinking of an eye. And, because of its particular connection with monks and pilgrims, it could therefore potentially speak in tangible terms of a spirituality that elsewhere had been lost or buried. To put this into words, MacLeod revisited the liturgies of the Celtic Church. But he was also a raconteur, and in his talks used to give a more immediate example of the 'Iona effect' from his own childhood as the son of a prominent Church of Scotland minister. 'When I was a boy of nine, we went over to Iona. My father said, "I think you should shake hands with Mrs McCormack. She's 85 years old." So I shook hands with Mrs McCormack, a little embarrassed. My father said, "Now I'll tell you why. When she was nine years old she shook hands with a Mrs Campbell who was then 85 years of age, and Mrs Campbell, when she was nine years of age, stood at exactly this point on the jetty and watched the boat going down the Sound of Iona taking Bonnie Prince Charlie back to France." Now that was a wonderful education – two hand-shakes away from Bonnie Prince Charlie!'

The time-span of my day-long journey is a blip against such huge sweeps of history, but I nevertheless foolishly cling to a sense of virtuousness on account of my efforts when I finally get to the abbey, deposit my bags in my bunk-bedded room, and sit down to dinner in what was once the medieval abbey's refectory. Around 60 other visitors have gathered for a three-day course – 'This is not a retreat' the literature warns in bold print – which attempts to step out of everyday living and give a taste of what it is like to share in the daily routine of prayer, work and worship of the Iona Community. Over shepherd's pie and water (the abbey doesn't permit alcohol) I find myself recounting my voyage with only the odd embellishment, to be politely trumped mile for mile, connection for connection, by individuals who have made their way here from Sweden, Norway, Germany, the United States and even – in a group of five – from an Anglican parish in Brisbane, Australia. It's another aspect, I reflect, ashamed into silence, of the extraordinary scale of tiny Iona.

*   *   *

Saint Columba was not, his legend suggests, a particularly easy man. There are, for example, plenty of references to his loud, rather insistent voice. When later I sit in the dusk outside the abbey next to Saint Martin's Cross, one of a handful of survivors of the reported 360 Celtic crosses that must once have crowded Iona, I wonder whether his voice was shaped by having to compete with an ever-present soundtrack on the island of the roar and swell of the Atlantic, clearly audible even on such a placid day as this. An old poet friend, who had served on the Orkneys as an officer in the Wrens during the Second World War, used to put her own astringent and occasionally off-putting voice down to struggling to convey orders against the wind that came uninterrupted all the way from the Arctic.

Columba – or Colm Cille, to give him his Gaelic name – was also said to be impatient and a hard task-master. The same charges were levelled against George MacLeod. Already, after such a short time on Iona, I'm getting the two mixed up. There is an informal, laughing, sparkly-eyed photographic portrait of MacLeod, taken in old age, that hangs just outside the Abbey refectory. It makes him look utterly benign, but he could be, as even his sympathetic 1990 biographer, Ron Ferguson, writes, 'what my aunty from Cowdenbeath would have called "an awfy man". And "awfy" could be awfy awfy – stubborn, imperious, insensitive, ruthless and manipulative.' MacLeod's admirers point out that these were precisely the character traits that made him realize what for others would have remained a dream – restoring a ruined abbey on a remote island not as an historical monument, or a draw for tourists, but as a living, breathing place of spiritual exploration and growth in the face of a rising tide of scepticism and secularism.

Columba's admirers, of course, praise the same vision and tenacity in their man. Like MacLeod, he made things happen. It was a quality that inspired his followers to look up to and love him. The Bay of the Coracle on the south-west tip of the island is reputed to be the natural amphitheatre where he landed in 563, though this is more best guess than historical fact. The pebbly shoreline is roughly in the right position if you draw a straight line over from Iona to the north coast of Ireland. And, as the name suggests, it is assumed Columba navigated the strong currents of the Irish Sea in the standard craft of the age, the coracle. With its shallow draft, it was designed, when propelled by oar or sail, to skate over currents and rip-tides.

There is an element of the *seanachaidh* – pronounced 'she-nach-ay' and Gaelic for storyteller or bard – in everything that is now told about Columba. Facts about him are few and far between. Yet out of such thin gruel, his legend has become a rich stew. Take the *Sithean Mor* – literally the 'smooth green

mound of fairies' – roughly in the middle of Iona. This is sup-
posedly the spot where Columba was observed by one of his
monks. While praying, he was visited by bands of angels in
white garments. The monk, who witnessed all this, had been
defying his leader's orders by following him, and so was duly
admonished by Columba for spying when he told the tale, but
it took wing nevertheless. The angels' presence is much
quoted, in hagiographies of Columba, as proof positive that he
was guided from above. So much so that later generations of
islanders decided to make the *Sithean* the place where they
would race their horses, carefully going round the course in
the same direction as the sun travelled. It is a perfect illustra-
tion of the ingredients of superstition, legend and belief that
flavour every corner of this compact, intense landscape.

Columba came over from Ireland, it is said, with 12 companions. Again there is a neat symbolism in the tale, with the
dozen helpers equating to the 12 apostles. There may have
been more, or there may have been fewer. Quite what inspired
him to make the crossing is equally vague. Columba did have
an official biographer in his descendant, Adamnan, who wrote
a life of the saint around 100 years after his subject's death in
597. The monks of Iona were, from the start, rather a talented
lot at writing things down and are believed to have done most,
if not all, of the work on the Book of Kells, the eighth-century
illuminated manuscript of the four Gospels regarded as one of
the masterpieces of Western calligraphy, and now kept in
Trinity College, Dublin. One theory holds that it was created
on Iona to mark the two-hundredth anniversary of Columba's
death and only later transferred, as a precaution in the face of
marauding Vikings, for safe keeping to the monastery at Kells
in County Meath that has given it its name.

Adamnan describes Columba as being 'fair, mighty form,
face ruddy, broad, radiant, body white, fame without false-
hood, hair curly, eye grey, luminous'. He says simply that
Columba went to Iona as a 'pilgrim for Christ' to convert the
heathen Picts. This was not virgin territory for Christians. Irish
travellers had started to colonize the west coast of Scotland

from the fourth century onwards, and in their wake had come missionaries. Much further south, for example, at Whithorn in Dumfries and Galloway, is the cave that was once the lonely hermitage from where, in 397, the Cumbrian-born, Rome-educated Saint Ninian evangelized. He built a church nearby – the Candida Casa, or 'White House', still a place of pilgrimage – and his mission is reputed to have spread over to the east coast and the Firth of Forth.

Most accounts suggest that Columba did not leave Ireland of his own free will. He was exiled. A descendant of the splendidly named royal prince, Niall of the Nine Hostages, Columba was, in this version, banished after a civil war that may or may not have been caused by his refusal to hand over to the king a copy he had made of the Gospel texts. The new life Columba set out to establish on Iona was, therefore, both punishment and atonement for past sins, up to and possibly including having blood on his hands. There could be, some claimed, no possibility of return to his birthplace. Columba is described in one ancient ballad as 'he who turned his back on Ireland'.

Yet this image of Columba as the repentant sinner cannot be pushed too far, for still other accounts of this riddle of a life state he was already a priest in Ireland before he left for Iona and had been living a virtuous life there, founding other monasteries at Derry and Durrow. Columba might also have been attracted by the presence on Iona of healing waters, the enigmatic Tobar na H-Aoise or 'Well of Youth' on Dun I, the highest point on the island. This spring is believed to have been known before Columba came. Might he have travelled there in search of healing after the battles of Ireland?

What is beyond dispute, though, is the impact Columba had on Western Christianity, and hence Western civilization once he got to Iona. The traditional map of the spread of Christianity shows all roads leading out of Rome. And indeed it was reportedly Pope Siricius who sent Ninian to Whithorn at the end of the fourth century, and later Pope Gregory the Great who despatched Augustine to southern England at the very end of the sixth century to convert the heathen King Aethelbert and establish a monastery at Canterbury. Yet by the time Augustine landed on the Isle of Thanet in 597 with 40 followers (another symbolic number in Christianity), Columba and his 'island soldiers', as Adamnan describes them, had spread out from their beach-head on Iona and won converts to their Celtic style of spirituality and worship all across Scotland and into northern England. Bridei, one of the kings of the Picts, was reputedly convinced in the mid-580s to embrace Jesus when he witnessed Columba drive away a man-eating 'water beast' from the river Ness by making the sign of the cross. The monster, Adamnan reports, reacted to Columba as if 'pulled back with ropes' and fled in terror. (Columba seems to have had a gift for getting rid of animals – Adamnan also tells how he banished snakes and frogs from Iona.)

After Columba died, his monks went from strength to strength, risking hazardous journeys, uncertain welcomes and, on occasion, open hostility in order to establish new monasteries. They preached their way through Europe, but Iona always remained a sacred place for them. Its enduring significance – for them and for subsequent generations – is perhaps best summed up by prophetic words attributed to Columba on his deathbed. 'Unto this place, small and mean though it be, great homage shall yet be paid, not only by the kings and people of the Scots, but by the rulers of foreign and barbarous nations and their subjects. In great veneration, too, shall it be held by holy men of other churches.'

The Celtic and Roman models of Christianity did not always co-exist easily – the first based on independent monasteries, preaching and the personal example of ascetic monks, with only the spiritual authority of individual abbots to give it form, the second increasingly structured, hierarchical, fond of rule-books covering every eventuality, and leaders keen to assert central control. Given their particular natures, it was inevitable the Celts would ultimately be subsumed into the Roman model. At the Synod of Whitby in 664 the process began in earnest, but it took until the twelfth century, scholars believe, for the imaginative and poetic theology that inspired Columba and those who came after him finally to be extinguished as a distinctive and distinguishable thread in Christianity.

*   *   *

After a fitful night's sleep in my bunk-bed – I'm too long for the downstairs berth and too tall for the gap between the top and the ceiling – I set off with my fellow visitors on a walk round Iona (one mile wide at its midriff by three-and-a-half long) to hear and see some more stories about Columba. History, geography and fiction mix effortlessly. At each stop, we pause a moment to say prayers and sing a communal alleluia drawn from different traditions around the world. The dash of spirituality tastes a bit odd at the start. The lingering effects of living in Western secular societies where religion tends to hide its light under a bushel is initially hard for the group to shake off, and our voices hardly ring out, but on Iona, gathering in prayer and song in the open air next to a Celtic cross has been going on unremarked upon for centuries. The ghosts of the past must be giving us courage for, soon enough, it becomes an entirely natural thing to do as our voices rise to the challenge of drowning out the sea and waves.

The course leader, Kathy Galloway, a smiley Church of Scotland minister and the first ever female head of the Iona Community (neither Columba nor George MacLeod were noted as forward thinkers, even by the standards of their time, on the role of women), has asked us to treat the pilgrimage round the island as a kind of 'road-to-Emmaus experience'. The reference is to the passage in Luke's Gospel where the resurrected Christ mixes with two of his disciples as they walk to Emmaus, a town near Jerusalem, but they do not recognize him. 'Try and see Christ in the stranger you are talking to,' Kathy urges us.

After a few awkward exchanges with members of a group of Swedish teenagers who have been brought by their saxophone-playing pastor on the course as part of their preparation for confirmation, I hit upon Nancy, a red-haired Presbyterian minister in her early fifties from Cincinnati. She is not, strictly speaking, a stranger, since we had spoken briefly the night before when we both arrived slightly late for the healing service, led by lay members of the community in the abbey church, and ended up taking the last two empty seats in the front row. I was uncomfortable being so exposed, but it was, Nancy had whispered to me, a blessing.

This morning, her vibrantly green hoodie stands out against the paler grass that grows in the sandy soil of the Machair – the common that gives onto what the locals call the Bay at the Back of the Ocean. This open space, our Iona community guide is explaining, used to be divided into strips and worked by crofters. Every year they would swap strips so each got a chance of the most fertile ones. 'So communal living has always been part of island life.'

The latest round of alleluias completed – 'This is from Korea,' explains our 21-year-old cantor Laura, an Anabaptist

Iona Abbey, seen from the organic vegetable patch.

from Indiana working at the Iona Community in preparation for a career in church musicianship – we start walking again. Nancy needs little encouragement to open up. This, she tells me, is her first-ever trip to Europe. Her only three previous journeys out of the United States have all been practical – getting her hands dirty helping set up missionary projects in Haiti, the Dominican Republic and Mexico. She is striding ahead at a cracking pace. The more reflective approach to Christianity on Iona is obviously leaving her with surplus energy.

So what brought her here? 'Well, I sometimes listen to the BBC on the net and one of my favourites is the religious talks given by John Bell from the Iona Community. So I figured I ought to come and hear him for myself.' Nancy, it turns out, is the veteran of our party, having been on Iona for nine days already, taking in the previous week's course run by Bell, another Church of Scotland minister, a regular on Radio 4's *Thought for the Day* and a well-known writer of hymns. 'I've known his music for such a long time,' Nancy adds, 'because I have always been very involved in our church choir, even before I was a minister.'

Bell's name – and that international audience for the music of Iona – has already been mentioned to me several times as the motivation for visitors coming here. The work of the Iona Community, once MacLeod's rebuilding really gathered speed in the post-Second World War years, was publicized by several means. The most obvious was MacLeod's own tours. He was a gifted speaker and a regular on the lecture circuit around the Commonwealth and the USA. He would return to austerity Britain having garnered enough overseas donations to complete the next stage of the reconstruction. But after MacLeod stood down as leader in the early 1970s (he died in 1991), it has principally been the distinctive music and liturgies devised by the Iona Community, drawing on Celtic traditions and melodies (Columba was also reputedly a decent hymnwriter) but using contemporary vernacular language to earth heavenly talk, that have really spread its reputation worldwide, striking a chord, especially among younger churchgoers.

Nancy is now telling me about her children – she has two, both teenagers and still practising Christians. Her husband is the sound technician in her church. Why didn't he come over too? 'He didn't need it as badly,' Nancy replies starkly, causing me to look at her afresh. He is, she continues, her second husband. The children's father was killed when her younger child was only two. 'It was tough,' she recalls. 'We didn't have any money.' Her smile, broad and saucer-shaped, never dips.

'But what about you, Peter?' she says as casually as if she is going to ask me one more time about my journey here. 'Where do you feel God's influence in your life?' The question strikes me dumb. It is one of those that you don't often get asked, save by the sort of street-corner evangelists Tony Blair no doubt had in mind when he explained his decision to keep quiet about his Catholic faith while Prime Minister in case anyone thought he was a 'nutter'. I begin and fail to complete several sentences. Nancy starts laughing. 'Oh, I am sorry.' She doesn't look it. 'I said the same thing to a man at the hotel I was staying at in Edinburgh' – she pronounces it Edin-burrow – 'and he told me that you just don't ask British people that.'

Perhaps there is an Iona effect at play here, something in the ether that draws such talk into the open. Dr Johnson noticed it in the eighteenth century when he wrote to his travelling companion and eventual biographer, James Boswell: 'That man is little to be envied . . . whose piety would not grow warmer among the ruins of Iona.' So I need only stay for a few more days and I will be as unabashed as Nancy. On the other hand, she might quite plausibly always be like this. 'I do like to be direct,' she confirms.

As if to prove the point, she shares a confidence. We are now walking alongside the wall that separates the path from Iona's primary school playground – current roll eight, two short for a five-a-side game of football. Her eyes fix on the lichen-encrusted stones that make up the wall and an old metal gate swinging on its hinges. 'Do you know,' she begins, 'I have always had three very clear pictures of myself in my mind all my adult life. One was of me sitting on a couch hugging my two children. It was only after my husband died that I realized he had never been in the picture. The second was of me in the church in Cincinnati where I am now a minister. It was the church I grew up in, so I had always assumed that it meant I was going to sing in the choir there. I'd never assumed it would be as the minister. But then it came true. And the third' – she gestures at the wall and gate – 'was a picture of me walking alongside an old wall and gate just like these. I always thought it might have happened in England when my first husband came over to graduate school, but then he died, and now here I am, and here are the wall and the gate.'

There is nothing tentative about the way Nancy tells it. On Iona, she has apparently found the final piece of a lifetime's puzzle. She believes she is somehow predestined to be here. Or has been directed here by God. This, then, is where *she* is feeling God's influence in her life.

*   *   *

What is it about islands and the Celts? Or, for that matter, islands and today's pilgrims? The walking tour is over and the schedule reads 'free time'. The questions are dancing around in my mind as I walk in the cemetery that surrounds Saint Oran's Chapel, at just shy of 900 years the oldest surviving building on the island. Such was the reputation of Iona in the centuries after Columba that 48 Scottish, eight Norwegian and four Irish kings are said to be buried here, the best known of whom, thanks to Shakespeare, is Macbeth. The most popular grave for visitors, though, is that of the 1990s Labour leader, John Smith.

All chose this spot, in the shadow of the abbey, looking out over the Sound, as their final resting place when anywhere would have been possible. It may simply have been for the view. A better one is hard to imagine. But then when you are six feet under, the view is not that important. The ancient kings also made their decision out of royal tradition and because, in their epoch, Iona would have been seen geographically as well as spiritually as a final stopping place on the road to the heavenly domain that lay just over the horizon in the land of the setting sun. John Smith, though, would have known that to the west lay America. Instead it was said at the time that, like many other visitors, he had valued in his lifetime the 'something other' about this island.

Islands have exerted down the ages a dream-like pull. 'Islomania', the poet, writer and traveller Lawrence Durrell called it in a letter to a friend in the 1950s. It is, he said, 'a rare affliction of the spirit. There are people who find islands somehow irresistible. The mere knowledge that they are in a little world surrounded by sea fills them with an indescribable intoxication.' He underestimated only the numbers of islomaniacs. They are not rare. Definitive Admiralty sea charts from the nineteenth century, for instance, include 200 islands now known not to exist but which had somehow crept onto otherwise rigorously policed maps, potentially as a kind of wish-fulfilment by lonely sailors, up in the bird's nest and so anxious to spot land that they reported seeing somewhere to port or starboard that existed only in their mind's eye.

Likewise Celtic folklore abounded with islands – some of them real like Iona, and some imagined. Saint Brendan's Isle was, according to legend, a place off the west coast of Ireland, visited by its namesake in 512, along with fourteen monks, who joined him in saying Mass before heading back to shore. It was never spotted again, and some have even questioned whether Brendan didn't, in fact, reach America almost a millennium before Columbus without realizing it. Then there was Hy-Brasil, often conflated with St Brendan's Isle, and again said to be located off the west coast of Ireland, and shrouded in mist on all but one day every seven years. It had been visited by other saints who returned to tell of this 'Fortunate Island', one of the several 'Blessed Isles' that, they claimed, were akin to stepping-stones linking heaven to earth.

While deserts and mountains may symbolize our fears in the face of nature – and, for some, the instinct to battle with nature or abandon themselves to its whims – islands are about escape, isolation and the search for a lost simplicity and wisdom, somewhere insulated from the rest of the world by encircling water, a place where what has been misplaced elsewhere has managed to remain largely untouched by modernity.

But while many now project their longings onto the island that is so associated with Columba, can those longings also be attributed to him? The Celtic myth of islands would have been known to him, but, rather than romantic or mystical, his decision to base himself on Iona is better seen as practical. Sea travel was, in the sixth century, regarded as safer than the alternative of going overland. So better make your base on an island just off the mainland, than on the mainland itself. Boat journeys were direct and their perils were, by and large, known. On land, you would be prey to any group you stumbled across.

Yet that can hardly be the whole story. Something in Columba reacted to Iona. Part of the Celts' fondness for islands lay in their belief that God might better be invoked and encountered in wild places, away from other inhabitants, in what might be called edgelands. The inspiration for this again came from the Desert Fathers, those Christian monks who from the third century onwards chose to follow the example of Jesus in the Gospels by retreating into the wilderness of the Egyptian desert. There they lived as hermits, doing hard manual labour and focusing their thoughts and prayers on God, their inner spiritual landscape augmented by a harsh outer landscape that challenged rather than contained the distractions of inhabited places. Later, when some of these desert monks began to gather in monasteries, they did so as individuals, each in their cells, living in silence and prayer, joining only for worship and food.

This was the model adopted by Celtic Christians. They therefore had a strong sense of nature being shot through with the spirit. By his death and resurrection, Christ had, they believed, redeemed not just humankind but the whole created order. They regarded nature – especially untamed, unpolluted nature, as found on islands – with a profound reverence.

That spiritual sense was later lost by the mainstream Church and indeed by society at large as the planet became seen simply as a resource to be exploited. Humankind were consumers – not an attractive word, evoking the image of gobbling up – of the world's resources rather than temporary custodians, or putty to be shaped by the experience of nature in the raw. Perceptions are now, however, once again shifting. The threat of climate change has given a new immediacy – and a renewed popularity – to that earthy holiness of the Celts, the memory of which has survived in the landscape of Iona.

Its tightly drawn natural borders and its status as a place at the start or end of a journey have both protected it. In a more transitory location, with travellers forever passing through, spiritual and historic deposits can easily be plundered and lost. Islands, though, make for better custodians – think Elba and Napoleon, Pitcairn and the *Bounty*, Shackleton and South Georgia. Once Iona may have been at the centre of missionary activity, but for much of its subsequent history it has been remote from the centres of power and influence and affluence, thus preserving an ancient sensibility that might otherwise have given way to industrialization, commercialization and precisely the modern pressures that many now come here to escape from.

*   *   *

Iona and the Iona Community are often treated as one, but there is more to the island for the spiritually hungry than the world of the abbey. Rising from my bunk-bed while the rest of the group are still asleep, I go on a solo pilgrimage in silvery blue early morning sunshine. Harry Cory-Wright, the Norfolk-based landscape photographer, takes all his shots, revealing the ethereal in the everyday, at sunrise rather than sunset. 'Early morning', he says, 'is a very special moment. When the sun rises, it catches something. It feels blessed. You are half asleep, dreamy, and there are prospects, uplift, celebration. Sunset, by contrast, is more sentimental, because it is looking back.'

Even in the sea breeze, with gannets and the sea circling,

there is a stillness about Iona that manages to rise from land-scape into your bones. As the single-track road heads north from the abbey towards the lonely cross erected in 1878 by the island's then owner, the Duke of Argyll, in memory of his wife, it requires little imagination to think myself into the sandals of the monk who defied orders and followed Columba as his leader set off in search of solitude and prayer. There will be no host of heavenly angels this morning, I feel pretty sure, but otherwise 1,500 years of human development have wrought few changes on this rocky moonscape. The Hill of the Seat, according to the legend, was a favourite perch of Columba and, once again, I cannot fault his sense of place. Directly below are the white sands of Traigh Ban; on the eastern horizon are the hills of Mull, baring their shoulders in the shadow of the cone-shaped peak of Ben More; and to the south east, on the other side of the Sound, the tidal islet of Erraid, used by Robert Louis Stevenson as the prison that traps Davie Balfour in *Kidnapped*, but today one of the bases of the Findhorn Foundation, founded in 1962 as another experiment in community living around shared – though not in this case exclusively Christian – values. There is something about this landscape that has been encour-aging idealism for centuries.

I retrace my route to the abbey but am still far too early for breakfast, so continue on into the village that surrounds the jetty. The abbey is just one of several houses of God on Iona. There is a plain, rectangular box of a kirk, designed by Thomas Telford, better known as a pioneering civil engineer. In MacLeod's early days, the minister objected loudly and repeatedly to what he saw as heresy at the abbey. The ecu-menism of MacLeod's plans offended in particular, which is not so surprising in the climate of the times, but it did sink to comical depths. In the local paper, a letter of complaint appeared about the offence being caused by the unemployed young men MacLeod brought over from Glasgow to carry out the rebuilding and their habit of hanging out their washing on a line near the abbey site. Sometimes, the correspondent reported in high dudgeon, the items had been spotted flapping in the wind on the Lord's Day. (MacLeod unexpectedly reaped a rich harvest from this small-mindedness when a cheque for £5,000 arrived with a note explaining that the donor had read the letter in the paper, disagreed with it, and wanted instead to applaud this practical demonstration that cleanliness is next to godliness.)

Further down my dawn pilgrim route, away off behind the primary school, slumbers a Catholic retreat centre, a long, white, extended bungalow, with its own chapel, which, according to the noticeboard outside, also runs residential courses. Columba and his island are bigger than any one denomination and venture, yet the existence of this separate Catholic venue contains a particular irony, for MacLeod was regularly regarded by many in his own Church as being far too 'popish'. And, indeed, in pursuit of his ecumenical goal, he even went, on one occasion, to visit the Pope in the Vatican, causing cries of astonishment among many of his co-religionists. Yet he never quite managed to surmount differences in attitudes to the Eucharist

'There is a stillness about Iona that manages to rise
from landscape into your bones.'

and therefore was unable, as he wished, to see Catholics fully participating in Communion services at the abbey.

There is still a dominant pan-Protestant feel to the Iona Community – or at least to my experience of it. I discover over the days of my stay at the abbey almost every variety of mainstream non-Roman Christianity represented. As well as Nancy's Presbyterianism and the Anabaptist background of Laura, the song-bird of yesterday's pilgrimage, I spend one breakfast sitting next to a young Anglican vicar from the Church in Wales who, in her own words, 'has a thing about islands'. That same night at supper, opposite me at the table are a German couple, workers in the community, Dorothea in housekeeping, and her husband, Hagan, an assistant in the kitchen, both of whom came over on the recommendation of their Lutheran pastor. In between meals, I fall into conversation in the common room with Audrey, a Methodist minister from inner-city Bristol, on sabbatical and indulging a lifelong desire to come to Iona. And, that morning, in the kitchen I talk to a Mennonite from Canada who, with his wife, takes two months each year out of the gentle life of retirement and grandchildren to volunteer in a Christian community. Last year, he tells me, he and his wife were with a group in Georgia, in the southern United States, which attempts to integrate recent Hispanic arrivals in America better into the local landscape. Next year, they are off to Arizona to work as classroom assistants with a residential community tackling mental health issues.

The rebuilding of community, attempting to exorcise the post-Reformation ghosts to make the churches once more fit for purpose in the modern world, was as important to MacLeod as the rebuilding of the abbey itself. Put people together, living, praying and undertaking practical tasks, and all denominational differences will soon fade, he believed, allowing the acres of common ground in regard of social justice and peace to bear fruit. So every guest on a residential course at the abbey is assigned to a team for community 'chores'. I am put with the Seals (as opposed to the Otters or the Puffins) and, once I have got over the sense of being transported back to the cub pack of my youth, take on breakfast preparation, from toast-making to laying, hosting and clearing a table in the refectory, and then, when the washing-up is done, vegetable chopping. I have, I am told as I work my way through a pile of carrots and turnips, landed the cushy option. The Otters are off cleaning the communal toilets and showers. One visiting ecclesiastical bigwig once asked MacLeod, as they scrubbed away with the toilet brush, why the abbey couldn't employ people to do such menial work. 'To prevent you doing what I did for eight years in Glasgow,' MacLeod shot back, '*talking* about the dignity of labour.'

What is conspicuously missing in the abbey community is anyone from outside the churches. Perhaps inevitably. The Iona Community's reputation has spread principally through church networks. One fan described the phenomenon: 'It was as if George MacLeod had swung on a bellrope at Iona Abbey and the sound had been heard in distant parts of the world.' Those who make the journey to hear the bells at first hand, however, have already made a Christian commitment, and are seeking to renew, refresh or reassign it.

The Iona Community does, to be fair, offer an open door and warm welcome to day-trippers and those staying in the island's hotels, bed-and-breakfasts and hostels, to join its Morning and Evening Prayer services. This is its outreach. But, as Laura admits when I ask about it, few take up the offer. Which is a shame, for Iona has managed to fashion out of past and present a beguiling and inclusive liturgical style that catches the rhythms and echoes of the island.

In another resonance of its Celtic past, prayer frames the beginning and end of each day at Iona Abbey. The words of an old friend come back to me as we settle after supper into our seats in the abbey church. 'Just think,' she remarked after we had been to the cinema to see *Into Great Silence*, Philip Gröning's 2005 documentary film about the life of Carthusians in a remote corner of the French Alps, 'there is always a group of monks or nuns somewhere around the world praying for you. So when I wake up in the middle of the night and can't

The past frames the present on Iona.

get back to sleep, I know I am not alone.' This is Iona's distinctive contribution to that global 24-hour service.

Fully-fledged members of the community – those who have made a commitment to a common discipline of daily prayer, reading from the Bible, mutual accountability for use of time and money, and action for justice and peace – are few in number here. There are only 270 of them worldwide and they have to go through a two-year period of preparation. At any time only a handful are actually resident on Iona. For practical purposes, the main base of the community is now in Glasgow, from where it runs its publishing operation and work on social justice. Of the community I have joined temporarily, the warden, the Revd Malcolm King, an Anglican vicar, is a full member. Kathy, our course leader, is another. As are Zam, a colourful and colourfully dressed United Reformed minister who works with the homeless in Brighton and has been telling slightly off-colour jokes at a relaxed early-evening open mike session, and her pony-tailed, rainbow-sweatered husband, David. 'I've never lived here,' Zam says when we get talking. 'This is like the mother house that members come back to for refreshment, a bit like the Franciscans.'

With so few full members around, the resident Iona Community is made up very largely of volunteers and paid workers, though the line between the two is blurred. Laura was once a volunteer but has returned for six months as a paid member of the support staff. And Elizabeth, the young housekeeper from Glasgow whose job is to make sure all visitors have enough blankets and hot-water bottles, gets a wage, but explains, while supervising the distribution of porridge by the Seals at breakfast, that she doesn't do it for the money. 'Where else would you get the chance to write your own liturgies?' she asks.

Tonight's is being led by Sally, a young, dark-haired woman with eyes downcast in prayer as she waits in an outsized wooden chair in the centre of the abbey church. The stones, reclaimed from old boundary walls, had been almost pinkish earlier in the sunlight, but at this late hour, illuminated by candles, they take on a purply hue. For such a fortress against the elements and, in past generations against ship-bound invaders, the abbey has a remarkably soft inside. A long, coloured drape, with stripes of warm apricots and reds, encircles the candlesticks on the plain stone altar and then stretches out towards the congregation in apparently casual, but no doubt carefully arranged, ridges.

One of the battles MacLeod had to fight with his colleagues in the Church of Scotland was over the degree of ornamentation in here. There is nothing stark or puritan about the setting, and nothing that excludes any denomination. So, for example, in the cloisters next door – each arch supported by delicate honey-coloured pillars that show the inner beauty behind the rugged exterior of the abbey – stands a bronze statue of the Virgin Mary emerging from a vast heart by Jewish sculptor, Jacob Lupchitz.

The services follow a weekly pattern of themes. Tonight, it is healing. There is to be a laying-on of hands, we have already been told by Kathy. 'Nothing to be nervous of,' she explains. 'It's a bit like giving you a hug.' It sounds like a licence for exuberance and excess, but instead there is an overwhelming solemnity – the words and movements of the healing rite carefully chosen to focus minds rather than excite.

Finding formulas of words that stress the shared beliefs of participants from all sorts of Christian traditions can be reductive, ending up with a bland lowest common denominator, but the Iona approach is more ambitious. 'Any fool can write learned language,' the Christian apologist C. S. Lewis once remarked, 'the vernacular is the real test. If you can't turn your faith into it, then either you don't understand it or you don't believe it.' Here the vernacular retains both its clarity and its reverence. 'Spirit of Unity, go-between God,' our facilitator begins. 'We have come on journeys of our own, to a place where journeys meet,' we respond, reading off a sheet. 'Creator of the world, eternal God,' she intercedes. 'We have come from many places for a little while,' we reply. 'Redeemer of humanity, God-with-us.' 'We have come with all our differences, seeking common ground.'

We get up and sit down, sing and are silent, within a framework that is simple, moving and appropriate for the setting and its history. As hands are placed gently and encouragingly

Iona Abbey – rugged on the outside, soft inside.

on the shoulders of those who come forward for the prayers of healing, I feel on my own the hand of the past resting just as lightly but unmistakeably.

7

Lindisfarne

For with the flow and ebb, its style
Varies from continent to isle;
Dry shood o'er sands, twice every day,
The pilgrims to the shrine find way;
Twice every day the waves efface
Of staves and sandelled feet the trace.
              'Marmion' (Canto II) by Sir Walter Scott (1808)

The signs are legion as I approach the hump on the Northumberland coastline that faces Lindisfarne. Pinned to lampposts, waste bins and even tree trunks, they show bobbing in the sea the Barbour-green roof of the sort of 4×4 favoured by city folk to navigate those treacherous urban crescents. This image, capable of making every car owner wince, is overprinted with garish writing which announces (without punctuation), 'Warning this could be you please consult tide tables'. Lindisfarne, you see, is a part-time island, between and betwixt continent and isle, as Walter Scott had it, or, to go back further to the eighth-century monk, scholar and Tyneside local lad the Venerable Bede in his *Ecclesiastical History of the English People*, 'an island in the strict sense of the word only twice a day, when cut off by the tide'.

It has arguably been even less of a 'proper' island since 1966, when a mile-long metalled road was opened, anchoring it to the mainland in another demonstration of humankind's obsession with showing nature who is in charge. Yet even this feat of civil engineering is only open until three hours before the high tide and from three hours after. The rest of the time it – along with the mudflats or Slakes which separate island and

154

coastline – is covered with salt water, which must play havoc with the tarmacked surface and push up maintenance bills. Your average suburban street will need resurfacing once a decade. This link to Lindisfarne – or shackle according to many of the remaining 162 islanders who bemoan the summer hordes it carries across like a conveyor belt – must require a fresh coating of tar once a year if it is not to disintegrate into the informal, muddy cart track it replaced.

Maybe it is in an effort to keep down other costs associated with the road that there is no barrier or flashing lights to stop you driving beyond the end of the land and out onto the Slakes just when the sea is streaming in. In our health and safety-conscious age, it is a curious omission. The warning signs, graphic as they are, seem inadequate at a time when every cyclist wears a helmet, every primary schoolchild brings a mandatory cap on sunny days, and news reports contain regular warnings of flashlight photography.

The only concessions to our risk-averse culture on the tidal road to Lindisfarne are the aged refuge boxes, peculiar, off-white, wooden garden sheds, on stilts and with a ladder up the front. They look like a child's drawing of a tree house but with the tree rubbed out. In this utterly flat but treacherous sea/landscape, pitted with channels and quicksands, they are the equivalent of static lifeboats for those cast adrift by the incoming tides, a place to scramble above the waves, once you have abandoned your 4x4 to the elements, and await the arrival of a rescue helicopter.

Lindisfarne benefits from that connection between holiness and islands already seen at Bardsey and Iona, but it uniquely spells it out. 'The Holy Island of Lindisfarne' reads the brown tourist roadsign, directing visitors off the main A1, using a formula first employed by pilgrims in medieval times to distinguish their destination from any another island that people might want to walk to. And, as with any name with more than three syllables, this ungainly formula has been subsequently abbreviated – to Holy Island or Lindisfarne, but rarely both.

Its twin names cover a range of possibilities. Lindisfarne has a romantic Celtic ring, anchoring it with Iona, Bardsey and other strongholds of early Celtic Christianity and its charismatic itinerant monks. Holy Island has a more precise, what-it-says-on-the-tin, Anglo-Saxon air, and reflects the island's subsequent success, after the landmark Synod of Whitby of 664, in following that gathering's dictates and mixing those Celtic roots with a more formal Roman Christianity to produce an unrivalled centre of scholarship, evangelization and pilgrimage.

Again, as with those other holy islands, there is that element of risk in getting to Lindisfarne that was and remains an essential part of the allure. The unmanned tidal road is just the latest manifestation of that tradition. You have always had to step beyond what is comfortable to get there. The *quid pro quo* is that by making yourself vulnerable, and, please God, surviving (albeit thanks to the refuge boxes in the case of the driver in the warning signs), you are somehow laying yourself open to a new experience. Your guard is down.

That has been at the core of Lindisfarne's story since the 630s when the newly installed King Oswald of Northumberland sent word to Iona, where he had once lived in exile when a mere prince and the victim of court intrigues, to plead with them to send a missionary south to his royal coastal fortress at Bamburgh so as to take up the work of converting his subjects to Christianity. The first to answer the call was Corman, but he decided quickly that his seed was falling on barren ground. He turned tail and returned to western Scotland with horror stories of 'uncivilized people of an obstinate and barbarous temperament'.

Undeterred by such warnings, another of the Iona Community, Aidan, stepped forward to take up the challenge, promising to offer Oswald's subjects, Bede writes, 'the milk of simpler teaching'. Arriving around 635, he was named a bishop by the saintly Oswald and offered his pick of sites on which to build a new monastery. No doubt perversely in the eyes of Oswald's courtiers, he opted for an uninhabited island known as Lindisfarne – literally 'retreat' ('farne') from or in the Lindis, the small tidal river that emptied into the sea around it. From the ramparts of Bamburgh Castle, Aidan could see it sitting a few miles off the coast to the north, amid 5,000 acres of tidal mud.

He made his choice, it was reported, because monks liked islands, and Lindisfarne in particular reminded him of Iona. The first bit is undeniably true, especially in the Celtic tradition, but it is hard today, as I pull over in a lay-by and stare out at Lindisfarne, to spot any resemblance to Iona. Yes, both are islands, but the Cheviot Hills that shadow the Northumberland coastline are rolling and fleshy in contrast to the craggy, boney landscape of Mull that continues over the sound into Iona. And Lindisfarne itself is low, soft and axe-shaped, a long handle of sand dunes running up to a huddled village on the blade.

There must surely have been more pragmatic reasons for Aidan's choice. The island was close, but not too close, to Bamburgh. Though political and spiritual co-existed more cosily back then than today, it wasn't a seamless garment. Celtic monks still appreciated the value of breathing space from the seat of kingly power. Moreover it was uninhabited, so could be made into whatever Aidan wished, without reference to local sensitivities. It came without a past. And the limited tidal access – there was a six-mile route over from Bamburgh on the Fenham Flats but it was notoriously tricky and required local fishermen as guides – could provide valuable respite and even a deterrent if the king or his successors became too insistent.

Whatever Aidan's motives for planting his cross on this physically unprepossessing island, he immediately set about building a wooden church on an elevated site at the south end of Lindisfarne on what is today known as the Heugh. His successors enlarged it into an abbey and monastery as the island's reputation grew. The most celebrated of these was Cuthbert, still a saint with popular recognition in the north of England. As first Prior at Lindisfarne and subsequently its bishop in the last third of the seventh century, he was a holy man whose reputation as a scholar, preacher and healer drew crowds to 'his' island. After his death in 687, his stone coffin, containing his perfectly preserved body, was one of the wonders of the age. It was reputed to have the power to effect miraculous cures and proved an even more powerful magnet for medieval pilgrims than the Lindisfarne Gospels, peerless late-seventh-century illuminated manuscripts produced by the island's monks and now in the British Museum.

Visitors back then had no 'safe' road. Some accounts even speak of the high-born who travelled across the flats on the backs of fishermen. It would have been a long piggy-back, but not as long as if they followed the circuitous route today's highway takes over the Slakes. It makes a dash over the narrowest bit of mud, then clings on, by its fingertips, to the long handle of sand dunes in order to arrive at a huddle of buildings on the far end of Lindisfarne. Instead, pilgrims of previous ages would have headed out bare-foot from what is still the preferred embarcation point on the mainland – Beal Sands – in a straight and purposeful line towards the Priory, taking whatever obstacles and snares nature threw up in their stride. If they were fearful, they had only to lift their eyes from searching out runnels to gaze at the near horizon where the abbey and monastery buildings on the skyline would have acted as a spur to press on.

This Good Friday the Slakes are shimmering silvery grey in the thin lemony mid-morning sunlight. As I park at Beal Sands, a line of 20-feet-tall wooden poles, driven into the mud and encrusted with barnacles (but no warning signs) stretches out in front of me carrying my gaze all the way to Lindisfarne. They stake out the ancient 'Pilgrims' Way'. It is this time-honoured route rather than the road that I am about to walk. My companions will be 100 or so others who have been heading here on foot for the past week from various parts of northern England and southern Scotland, in five separate groups, each carrying a life-size cross. They are part of Northern Cross, an ecumenical group, largely Christian but not exclusively so, that on this anniversary of Christ's death on the cross stages an eye-catching act of

Lindisfarne is an island in the strict sense of the word
only twice a day.

witness that culminates in a traditional bare-footed crossing
to Lindisfarne.

Theirs has already been a gruelling hike – 12–15 miles a day,
usually on footpaths but occasionally with no option but busy
roads and dodging the traffic, with nights spent on the floors
of church halls in sleeping-bags, with minimal bathroom facil-
ities and only such sustenance as can be rustled up between
a long day's slog and soaking your blisters. And on top of all
this there is the shared responsibility of shouldering a wooden
cross. So why do it?

It is a mark of how out of touch our age is with religion and
spirituality that the question requires some thought. In pre-
Reformation times pilgrimages such as Northern Cross were
commonplace, their demands well understood by participants
and observers alike as groups trudged along the lanes and
byways of Britain. Today, to the casual motorist driving past,
they are regarded as displays of impenetrable masochism.

National newspapers have in the past run side-by-side in their Holy Saturday editions a moody picture of the Northern Cross stalwarts on the Slakes with a shot of the annual Good Friday ceremony in the Philippines, where extremist Catholics nail themselves to a cross in commemoration of Jesus's death. The juxtaposition of the two images suggests an equivalence between the two.

Walking long distances, Northern Cross's chosen act of remembrance is, in one sense, a kind of punishment, but it is based on a simple and (almost) universal physical function. We hold ourselves upright, and tense our muscles so as to move one leg then the other. Yet the scientific definition just doesn't really cover it. There are, for starters, the very different ways in which we move our legs. Everyone has a walk – long strides or tiny steps, rapid paces or languid gait, toes in, toes out, heels first, heels last, knees knocking, knees gaping. Every style tells a story about the person. Moreover, it is only when we can't make this apparently unremarkable muscular reflex of walking that we begin to appreciate how essential it is to life. My mother's multiple sclerosis was like a wave breaking slowly but inexorably up over her body from her feet, drowning functions from her toes onwards as methodically as a night watchman going round a deserted office building switching off the lights. She craved from her wheelchair one exemption more than any other – to retain the ability to take just one step, the one step that would carry her unaided from bed to chair, from chair to car seat, from chair to toilet.

Her unanswered prayers were a part of my childhood. So I realized early on that walking should never be taken for granted. Most of us, though, come eventually to the same realization and recognize that putting one foot in front of the other, along with other basic functions such as eating and breathing, is invested with a whole variety of meanings. At its simplest, as we grow into adults and lose the natural vitality of childhood, we learn to appreciate the health-giving qualities of a 20-minute brisk walk. And as citizens, we can make our voices heard by the act of walking in procession to demonstrate against the policies of our government. Walking takes on a political power.

It can also be an act of reflection. The American essayist Rebecca Solnit writes in *Wanderlust*, her history of walking: 'Walking itself is the intentional act closest to the unwilled rhythms of the body, to breathing and the beating of the heart. It strikes a delicate balance between working and idling, being and doing. It is a bodily labour that produces nothing but thoughts, experiences, arrivals.'

What Solnit so eloquently identifies, pilgrims down the ages have always known. Taking on an arduous, physical labour in the form of a long or treacherous walk can help you to access a spiritual dimension shut off during the everyday routine. But it has to be hard. No gentle stroll in the countryside will suffice. The origins of the word 'travel' – in *travail*, or work – suggest that it should not be the effortless cruise or the door-to-door service of holiday company brochures, but rather a sustained and purposeful effort.

Christianity has had a tendency, of course, to take that effort to extremes – encouraging pilgrims to trek long distances in bare feet, or with stones in their shoes, or to ascend on their knees the Scala Santa, or 'holy staircase', in Rome's St John Lateran Basilica. The essential point, though, remains not one of degree but of purpose. There is a conscious effort in the *travail* of walking to make the spiritual tangible – not necessarily by inflicting pain on the body, though again there is a long history of bodily mortification in the churches (carried on to this day in such dark corners of modern Catholicism as Opus Dei with its penchant for self-flagellation, as flamboyantly highlighted in Dan Brown's *The Da Vinci Code*), but rather by the repetitive act of walking over such an extended and sustained period as to allow the individual to transcend the pain barrier and find an affinity with his or her body that makes the physical irrelevant and thereby releases the mind for higher thoughts. If the landscape in which the pilgrimage takes place is one that positively encourages such higher thoughts, then so much the better, because it creates a consonance between the internal and the external. The mudflats to Lindisfarne neatly fit the bill.

All of which the walkers gathered with me on Beal Sands know better than I do. There is a hard core that return year after year. It all started in 1976 with a group of students. They had been on a similar pilgrimage to Walsingham in Norfolk, recalls one of the founder members, Ken Williams. 'We decided', he recalls, looking me straight in the eye, 'that we wanted to walk somewhere that's prettier. Norfolk's very nice but very flat. When you are walking with a cross and the big event of the day is turning a corner, you need to look elsewhere. We thought of Iona but it was just too remote. And then we thought about Lindisfarne, discovered there was a hostel there where we could stay, and here we are.'

Ken has been coming back almost every year since, accompanied by his wife Catharine. They are pilgrimage *aficionados* who met while on the 'Camino' across northern Spain to the shrine of Santiago de Compostela. Pinned to their sweatshirts and hats are the small white and red crosses that have been handed out on previous Northern Crosses – red for Christ's suffering and death, and white for his resurrection. 'It gets compelling,' Ken admits. 'Your feet start getting itchy around Easter time. The years I didn't do it, I found myself walking up and down the garden singing *Avanti Populo* at the top of my voice.' Each leg has a small booklet that participants carry, with daily hymns and readings – plus the occasional marching song. Ken breaks into a chorus of *Avanti Populo*. He gestures at me to join in, but I've never heard it before. 'Don't you know it?' he asks, breaking off abruptly. 'It's an Italian nationalist song. You don't hear it in churches that often, but it's great for walking.'

The large wooden crosses are piling up, propped against a road sign on Beal Sands, as each of the five legs arrives to cheers and applause. They are no sooner over the finishing line of this marathon than they discard – for the time being – their burden. As the pilgrims reconnect with old friends from other legs after a year's absence, they seem initially determined to play down any spiritual side to their endeavour. There's much talk of the comradeship, of the joy of seeing familiar faces year after year, of stopping off at pubs on the route, even of a picnic on the leg that sets off from Lanarkshire at the gates of Traquair House in Peeblesshire, once a stronghold of Bonnie Prince Charlie. But what about the faith element?

'Its not a Holy Roller group,' Jan, a writer in her fifties from Edinburgh, gently rebukes me. 'When I tell my friends I'm going to Northern Cross, and that they do carry a cross, they say, "Oh my God, it's like Monty Python." The first time I came, I told myself that I would make an excuse and go home, that I just couldn't walk along the road carrying a cross. Completely no. But soon after we set off, someone in my group got a big blister and I found myself thinking, why am I standing outside myself watching myself do this? I've done Carnival in Rio. There comes a moment when you stop thinking about what other people think of you, worrying that you are part of a group of Christian nutters, and realize instead that they are just a bunch of nice people walking along.'

I move among each group of new arrivals, struggling to extract anything spiritual. Eventually it dawns on me that I am being too direct, too prescriptive. This is a pilgrimage that prefers to let its crosses do the talking. Maggie Mason is another veteran, a town planner by trade, a cradle Catholic who has joined the Methodists, the mother of grown-up children and Ken's sister-in-law. She is chief organizer this year – an elected role decided by a ballot on Lindisfarne at the end of the previous year's event. 'Its physical and it's a physical witness,' she reflects when I ask her why participants are so reluctant to distinguish between what they are doing and the Ramblers' Association. 'I think it is a prophetic act. Jesus did a lot of prophetic acts, like riding into Jerusalem. He did things where people could work out what he meant, but he didn't necessarily have to explain it. So we walk and we carry a cross and we develop our understanding of it as we walk and as we experience it.'

I point to the cars passing us on their way to Lindisfarne.

This is both low tide *and* a Bank Holiday, so there is a steady stream of traffic. Their passengers are staring at the crowd and the pile of outsized crosses, but not in a way that convinces me they readily understand what is going on. 'We walk through villages with our cross on our shoulders,' Maggie says, 'and a lot of people wave because they love to see us every year. Some make us soup and sandwiches and ask us in to use their bathrooms. Others do look at us blankly and I suppose we don't do a lot of explaining. We only explain if people ask us questions. We don't evangelize.'

She breaks off to welcome the last of the five legs which has just arrived. They originally set off from Penrith in Cumbria and have been up since four this morning in order to make the rendezvous, but their respite is brief. The tide timetable makes few allowances for getting your breath back. It is time to set out across the sands. Ken is nonchalant. 'This is the easy bit. In some ways, the least important.' He must have seen my face fall. 'But in some ways the most important, because it is the final few miles. It's a bit like the Last Night of the Proms. It only means something if you have been through the whole season beforehand. It is a kind of end-of-term party.'

Maggie has now hauled herself up onto a grassy knoll to give last-minute instructions and stands with Lindisfarne as her backdrop. The Health and Safety Executive would be proud of her performance. Always keep to the left of the poles to avoid quicksand. Mind the cars on the first small stretch, shared by the road and the Pilgrims' Way. There's more practical stuff about the lunch that will await us on the other side, and the sleeping arrangements for the rest of the weekend, which Northern Cross will spend on Lindisfarne. And then finally, and unexpectedly, she issues a rallying cry that edges into a sermon.

'Jesus did not go back on what he did to escape his fate. He meant it right to the death. You guys have walked carrying the cross. You could have had a walking pilgrimage without carrying the cross, or a walking holiday, but you've carried the cross and it was hard but you've tried to live in the way that

The wooden posts mark the Pilgrims' Way to Lindisfarne.

Jesus taught us to. We've tried to share food and look after each other and ask forgiveness when we do something wrong. We don't go across the sands all dour and down. We will do that later. We go across happy. We laugh and sing and splash in the puddles. Use your imagination to see Jesus walking with us because I am sure that he is, and I am sure that he is delighted to be with us . . .' she leaves only the smallest of pauses to play to the gallery . . . 'weird bunch that we are.'

And so off we head. A couple of volunteers are waiting on the edge of the mudflats with bags to collect discarded footwear. In typical Northern Cross style, everyone is busy explaining to me that they are going barefoot because the salt water ruins the leather of their hiking boots. Perish the thought that it might be anything to do with imitating past generations of pilgrims who trod this same path.

The first contact between my sole and the brown, soft mud is decidedly strange. My body instinctively recoils, as if I were about to press my bare foot into a pile of dog droppings. When

I force it, the sensation is cold and unpleasant, but it's already too late to go back. Dirty feet cannot easily be forced back into socks and shoes. As I proceed timidly step by step on this unsteady surface, each foot sinks for a moment down through the top layer, and blacker, thicker, viscous mud oozes up between my toes, drowning them. In smart urban health spas, they would charge a fortune for this as part of a pedicure.

Once I've passed through the psychological barrier of getting my feet muddy – I could hardly call it pain – my mind turns to all the other footsteps that have gone before me on this pilgrim path. The same thought has been present, of course, at all the sites I have visited. The challenge has been to find a trace of what the centuries have usually covered to good effect. Here, at Lindisfarne, on the mudflats, it is harder still. For it takes not centuries but seconds for the imprint of feet to be erased. Anything that does linger will be washed away twice a day by the incoming sea. All is temporary, of the minute, starting again at 12-hourly intervals. Yet there are the poles that mark the path. They offer an exactitude that has arguably been missing elsewhere. There, I have been wandering around in the right general area. Here, I am literally following a straight line to Lindisfarne's past.

The seasoned walkers of Northern Cross set a cracking pace. Last year, one admits as he hurries past, they were caught in a snowstorm, so they have learnt not to dawdle. I try briefly to keep up, but find – even without a cross on my shoulder – that I am soon firmly in the middle of the pack. Faces appear at my shoulder, chat for a while, and then accelerate, or fall back. It sounds clinical but it isn't. It happens almost without me noticing, which is, I'm sure, what those rescued from the refuge boxes say about the incoming tide.

Mike Holliday is another Northern Cross veteran. We bond over being dilettantes on this year's pilgrimage. He could only manage to join up at Beal Sands this year, so we have both missed the full week-long build-up. What keeps him coming back? 'It does recharge the spiritual batteries because it takes you away for a week from the hustle and bustle of normal life.

Walking the Slakes with the cross in an act of witness.

There's still a certain amount of hustle and bustle obviously, in organizing 15 or 20 people moving across the country, but it's a different hustle and bustle.'

A particular challenge he recalls is the hostile reception his leg got on their travels one year. 'Some people there thought it might be a good idea to throw stones at us.' He says it in such a light-hearted way, I don't quite take it seriously at first. You might be puzzled by the sight of grown-ups walking through the countryside with a cross. You might even feel irritated by such a naked display of Christianity if you were a convinced atheist. But stoning? 'Who knows why they did it,' he says. 'We didn't stop to ask. But certainly they find us strange. This happened on the other side of the Scottish border, but we have also had it in Northumberland.' Did the route take them close to troubled estates, I ask? He laughs at the assumptions I am making. 'No, this was in the countryside. It has lots of kids with no notion of how to behave.'

The sun is steadily burning off the low cloud, giving the flats a mirror-like quality. There is not a sign of snow. Somewhere

out there are oyster beds. Lindisfarne appears as far away as
ever, but I decide there is no point trying to work out how far
there is still to go. In the group that catches up with Mike and
me at a particularly tricky runnel is a Muslim woman from
Turkey. Northern Cross is, I suggest to Cheedam, an unusual
place to end up for her. 'It was an advertisement I saw,' she
explains. 'I have been living in Britain for two years, studying
and working, and the thing that has puzzled me most about you
is that I just don't see faith here when I am going about my life.
I am returning home soon and wanted to find if there was any
before I go. This sounded like an opportunity of seeing it.' How
had she found the daily prayer and reflection sessions that begin
and end the day's walking? 'Interesting.' She sounds tentative.
'Some things I didn't understand at all. My family at home is
not very religious. But there were many overlaps with Islam.'

The pilgrimage, of course, also has a special place in Islam
and religions other than Christianity. For devout Muslims, the
hajj – or pilgrimage to Mecca – is the fifth pillar of Islam and
an obligation once in a lifetime if you are in good health and
can afford it. Three million travelled there in 2008. Mecca,
though, had been a centre of pilgrimage before Mohammed's
time. Islam sees the roots of the practice in the figure of
Abraham and the journey he and his family made (in Genesis
in the Old Testament/Hebrew Scriptures, and also in the
Qu'ran) to the land that God has promised him. Islam also has
a word for the state of being on pilgrimage – something
lacking in the Christian lexicon. *Ihram* describes both the
experience and the special dress that men are meant to wear. If
taking off your shoes counts as special dress, then I am mid-
Ihram.

Ahead of us the cross-bearers are stopping to exchange the
burden. There is a short pause to readjust the scarves tied
around the central joint as padding. 'It still sticks into your
shoulder blade,' Mike confides, 'but over the years the crosses
have got lighter.'

The age profile, though, has remained much the same.
There are plenty of younger people on the Slakes, many of

them the children of the original Northern Crossers. Franckie, who joins our group, has just returned from working in the Antarctic as a meteorologist, so she knows all about endurance in tough conditions. She first came on Northern Cross with her parents. 'When I got to 17 I thought, "I'm too cool for this" and lapsed, but by my fifth or sixth year at uni, I'd come back. I don't generally go to church week by week. I just don't. It's really inconvenient on Sunday morning, but I get a top-up here. Every year there are different people, a different mix, different songs, different jokes, but it is the same.'

The longer we walk, the less talking we do. It may just be conserving energy. Lindisfarne is starting to get bigger, but so is the effort required to lift feet out of the mud to make each step. The groups start to fragment. Individuals walk alone, with an air of not wanting to be interrupted. Those unable to abandon themselves to their thoughts gather round the cross-bearers who have started to sing. Not *Avanti Populo* yet, but sturdy hymns nonetheless that beat and sustain a rhythm and a sense of purpose.

*   *   *

The tidal road now controls which Lindisfarne you experience. When it is open, the island is flooded with visitors, but as the expiry date for 'safe period' crossing looms, there is a convoy of cars back to the mainland. The islanders breathe a sigh of relief and the atmosphere changes.

The three-and-a-half mile trek across the Slakes ended up taking a couple of hours. Warm bowls of water were awaiting us on the shores of Lindisfarne when we arrived for rinsing the mud off tired and tarnished feet. There was a small crowd, drawn by the sight of the crosses coming into view, and by the sound of the singing, but it quickly dispersed towards the car park to beat the incoming tide.

One minute the narrow grid of streets was full, now it is almost silent. Lindisfarne is an island again for the next eight hours. A lone lime-green Rover saloon is cruising around. The

The padding around the centre joint makes the cross
easier to shoulder.

couple inside look bewildered. Perhaps they are islanders
enjoying the uninterrupted use of their own roads, but I
suspect they have missed their chance to get back to Beal Sands
before night-time. Later I see them parked on the shoreline,
still inside their car, monitoring the water level as it laps up
over the first section of the road.

After a makeshift lunch, the Northern Cross pilgrims are
settling into their dormitories and preparing for an evening
service in Lindisfarne's modern Catholic church to commemo-
rate Good Friday. It is an ecumenical organization. More than
once, I have been told, 'There are only two rules about
Northern Cross. It is ecumenical. And there aren't any other
rules.' But the proximity of their hostel to the Catholic church
makes its use the practical option.

While they unpack, I wander off in search of Saint Cuthbert.
A shepherd boy, who Bede tells us entered a monastery after
seeing a vision of Aidan being carried to heaven by angels,
Cuthbert was for a short time a soldier before spending 12

years from 664 as Prior of Lindisfarne Abbey, celebrating Mass with – legend has it – tears in his eyes, and, through patience, piety and personal example, persuading this stronghold of Celtic Christianity to integrate with the Anglo-Saxon church. Some monks did leave Lindisfarne to return to their *alma mater* of Iona after the Synod of Whitby, including Bishop Colman, but Cuthbert remained. It was his scholarship, preaching and, above all, personality that made the island, in the words of the contemporary poet and chronicler of myth and legend, Kevin Crossley-Holland, 'a kind of Mecca, a Canterbury of the North, the brilliant focal point of a brilliant age'. When the tides permitted, he sent out Lindisfarne's monks to continue the work of evangelization, founding churches and centres of learning throughout Northumberland and beyond. And when they didn't, he set them to work in the stark, simple scriptorium of the abbey, filling the long hours by carving great standing crosses and producing delicate, lavish illuminated manuscripts that spread Lindisfarne's learning and name far and wide.

Inspired and inspiring though he was as a leader, Cuthbert longed to escape, and in 676 he finally decamped for Inner Farne, a tiny island to the south of Lindisfarne, now a bird sanctuary, where he built himself a cell and found peace as a solitary hermit. This self-imposed exile lasted for eight years. Despite turning his back on the world, his reputation remained and, in 684, he was named Bishop of Lindisfarne, now – as a result of the changes dating back to Whitby – part of the larger Archdiocese of York. He tried and tried to resist the call. 'Letters and messengers were sent to him repeatedly,' writes Bede, 'but he refused to move.' It took a visit from King Ecgfrith of Northumberland, who knelt at Cuthbert's feet in his cell on Inner Farne, to persuade him to change his mind. He lasted two years in post before contracting what is believed to have been tuberculosis, a diagnosis which allowed him to retire alone (for fear of spreading the infection) back to his cell to die in March 687. He was buried in a stone coffin at the right-hand side of the altar of the priory church on Lindisfarne.

Bathing sore feet after the walk.

As well as Inner Farne, Cuthbert had another favourite retreat nearer to the abbey – what is now called Saint Cuthbert's Isle, a rocky outcrop off the south shore of Lindisfarne. Here he would go alone to pray. It wouldn't have been exactly private. The monks would have been able to see him from the abbey church, but the tides protected him from them getting too close – as they protect the isle now as I walk along the Heugh and spot it. I can only stand and look out at it on the other side of a narrow strip of water. As I do, it strikes me that Cuthbert sounds rather like another more recent monk and son of the north east, the late Cardinal Basil Hume. Both had that air of holiness, of carrying God in their shadow and of holding high office reluctantly, under obedience to his God. Hume spoke often of his wish to retire to the peace of his Benedictine monastery at Ampleforth in north Yorkshire.

Cuthbert was regarded by many as a living saint, a much more straightforward concept in the first millennium of Christianity where saints emerged by popular acclaim rather than the system since, which involves a quasi-judicial appointments' process policed by the Vatican. He was especially popular, Bede writes, with 'the rough hill folk' who believed that Cuthbert could perform miracles and labelled him 'the wonder worker of England'. His powers reportedly manifested themselves – as was the case with many medieval saints and healers – in a particular bond with animals. Bede writes in his *Life of Cuthbert*:

He [Cuthbert] was in the habit of rising at dead of night, while everyone else was sleeping, to go out and pray, returning just in time for morning prayers. One night one of the monks watched him creep out, then followed him stealthily to see where he was going and what he was about. Down he went towards the beach beneath the monastery and out into the sea until he was up to his arms and neck in deep water. The splash of the waves accompanied his vigil throughout the dark hours of the night. At daybreak he came out, knelt down on the sand,

and prayed. Then two otters bounded out of the water, stretched themselves out before him, warmed his feet with their breath, and tried to dry him on their fur. They finished, received his blessing, and slipped back to their watery home.

It's a great story, with distinct echoes of Saint Beuno, fond of standing immersed in water at Holywell. And the conceit that all of this is only known because a monk was spying on Cuthbert reminds me of Columba and his encounter with angels. The notion of miraculous powers that are somehow hidden from daily view, and which can only revealed by accident, is a recurrent one in the medieval literature about saints.

If in life Cuthbert was popular, in death he became a phenomenon, the object of national veneration. Literally the object, when, eleven years after his death, his sarcophagus was exhumed and his body found to be intact. (One modern theory on this apparent miracle is that the dry, salty land of Lindisfarne had, in effect, naturally embalmed the body.) Thereafter pilgrims flooded in from far and wide in great numbers to the Lindisfarne Priory, bearing gifts and hoping for (and claiming to receive) miraculous cures through Cuthbert's intercession. In the 730s, Ceolwulph, King of Northumberland, exchanged his purple robe for the cowl of a monk and retired to Lindisfarne, in the process endowing it with many treasures.

The presence of such rich pickings in a spot that had no army to defend it, and only the tides for protection, attracted the seafaring Vikings who, it is to be presumed, had heard of Lindisfarne by repute. They were quite capable of navigating their way into the island's harbour, and did so in 793, their first raid on English soil, making off with gold and silver plate from the abbey, murdering those monks who stood in their way. They returned the next year, and the threat they posed continued to cast a shadow over Lindisfarne until, in 875, the Norsemen were once again spotted off the coast, heading for the island, having already plundered a monastery at Tynemouth.

The monks responded by taking what must have been an agonizing decision. They abandoned their island sanctuary, loaded up Cuthbert's body, the head of Oswald and the bones of previous bishops Aidan, Eata, Eadfrid and Ethelwold, along with manuscripts and whatever plate they still possessed, and headed off across the Slakes in search of a place of greater safety. After spells in Chester-le-Street and Ripon, Cuthbert's body finally arrived over a century later in Durham, where it remains to this day.

Meanwhile the church and monastery on Lindisfarne fell into disrepair and the pilgrims ceased to make the crossing. There was a brief return to glory in 1070 when, after the Norman Conquest, William marched north, intent on punishing the people of Northumberland for resistance to his authority. The monks feared for the fate of Cuthbert's remains and headed back with them to deserted Lindisfarne. It is reported that when the bearers reached Beal Sands, the waters miraculously opened, like the Red Sea in the Bible, to allow the island's adopted son to return home. It was, however, a brief stay. The next year, Cuthbert's body – still apparently intact – was back on its way to Durham. It was his final parting from Lindisfarne.

*   *   *

A gentle drizzle has started to fall and I begin to see how isolated this part-time island can feel when it is cut off from the mainland. Nine-tenths of it is made up of either barren sand dunes, covered with marram grass and potted with rabbit holes, or treeless, flat, marshy fields. On a warm summer's day, they might make a good place for a picnic or a nature ramble, but on an increasingly cold April Friday afternoon, they hold little appeal. I need shelter.

The ruins of the priory are cheek by jowl with the Anglican parish church of St Mary's, the latter modest and watertight. I stay for as long as it takes for the latest downpour to pass over before going over to the magnificent but roofless priory next door. It stands more or less on the spot where Aidan built his first church, but what remains bears no resemblance to what was here in Lindisfarne's golden age. The ruins post-date the height of the Cuthbert cult by more than two centuries. Ownership of what was left of the abbey was granted to a group of Benedictine monks from Durham. They established a community here in 1093 and consecrated their new church in 1120.

It was built of sandstone and has been described by architectural historians as Durham Cathedral on a smaller scale. It may be the effect of the grey light, but the heavy colouring of the stone does not readily lift the spirit. Sir Walter Scott, quoted earlier, used Lindisfarne Priory as one of the settings in his epic poem, *Marmion*, about the Battle of Flodden. He wrote of it as:

> A solemn, huge, and dark red pile,
> Placed on the margin of the isle.

And in fairness, it is still possible to see that, as well as size, it had flourishes to draw the crowds. Above what would have been the principal door, rows of zig-zag ornamentation remain, and the most extraordinary surviving fragment of all is a lofty arch, decorated again with zig-zag moulding, that stretches diagonally over what would have been the centre of the cross shape that was the church. It is known as 'the rainbow arch' and evidently used to support a central tower that survived the dissolution on the orders of Henry VIII in 1541, as well as use as a storehouse and even the stripping of the building by Lord Walden in 1613 (one of his boats, loaded with bells, lead and other booty, sank in what was taken as God's revenge) to still be there as late as 1750.

It was not only the rebuilt abbey that attracted pilgrims from the twelfth through to the sixteenth centuries. Many early illuminated manuscripts were brought back and put on display, but Lindisfarne was already a kind of living museum, trading on a glorious past, largely irrelevant to the contemporary church. It no longer even had its own bishop. And once the monks had finally gone, its inhabitants – as many as 600 in the nineteenth century – turned to fishing, mining and running limekilns. Only a handful of trawlers still operates out of the harbour.

Today, almost six centuries after it ceased to be a place of worship, the priory ruins feel curiously dead, offering no tangible connection to the past. Once the beating heart of Lindisfarne, they now compete for visitors with rival attractions. There is a brewery making mead and selling it as the monks' drink and even an aphrodisiac. And there is a stout sixteenth-century fairytale castle, built on a rocky outcrop at the other end of the axe blade from the priory, using stones looted from the derelict church. It used to be a fort, though never an important one, but its main claim to fame is that it was converted into a home at the start of the twentieth century by the architect of New Delhi, Sir Edwin Lutyens. He even roped in the noted gardener Gertrude Jekyll to make over the old walled vegetable garden which now sits, incongruously, a good way from the castle, in the middle of marshy fields.

One of the castle's National Trust custodians tells me that it now attracts more visitors than the priory itself, a sign that what was once uniquely attractive about Lindisfarne has been, at best, diluted. Eccentric castles are, in Britain, almost ten-a-penny. A history as the Canterbury of the North, a kind of Mecca, is not. Yet, even on Good Friday, that true significance of Lindisfarne in the history of faith in Britain appears if not lost, then certainly hazy.

A casual visitor here, unaware of its past, would find a place of austere beauty, of history, and of shifting sands, literally and metaphorically, but they might not sense in the carefully tended ruins some lingering sense of those holy monks and the marks they left behind. Like the footprints of pilgrims in the Slakes, I know they have been there, but I can't see them. Perhaps all I need is less rain, a sunnier day, or better still a context, such as Northern Cross.

Back in the church hall, they are preparing for an evening service. Catharine, Ken's wife, wants to know how I found

A resting place for crosses on Beal Sands.

Lindisfarne. When I confess my doubts, she looks thoughtful and then draws on her long experience of such journeys. 'Pilgrimages can be disappointing, you know. Once we went back to Santiago. It took us a month to walk there. When we arrived, it was a big feast day, but Franco was paying a visit, surrounded by guards. It changed everything. The whole thing was a real disappointment.' How did they cope? 'Oh, by knowing there will be other pilgrimages, other destinations. And, after all, it's the journey there that is important. That's when you make the friendships, gain the insights.'

8

Glastonbury

And did those feet in ancient time
Walk upon England's mountains green?
'Jerusalem', from the preface of
Milton: A Poem, by William Blake (c. 1808)

As I gaze out from the top of Glastonbury Tor, the dykes that far below radiate from its base to prevent the low-lying Somerset Levels from flooding are glinting in the May Day morning sunshine. Long, thin, and each containing a thread of silvery water, these drainage ditches, known locally as rhynes, look from my lofty vantage point, 531 feet up, like darning needles casually dropped by a giant whose feet once walked on the summit of the Tor.

Such images usually float away before they even register in the brain, much less prompt any further consideration, but this is Glastonbury and there is nothing usual about it. In this Somerset town, reality and legends have, for millennia, merged to create a place where anything is not just possible but plausible. Jesus is said to have headed here from Palestine in those blank years in the Gospels, the three decades between his circumcision and the start of his public ministry. That is believed to be the allusion Blake is making in 'Jerusalem'.

Another visitor was Joseph of Arimathea, after the crucifixion, carrying in his knapsack the Holy Grail, the chalice Jesus had used at the Last Supper. Then there was Saint Patrick before he made his name in Ireland. And Gwyn, king of the fairies. And King Arthur.

The hard evidence for any or all of these is non-existent, but that's to miss the point of Glastonbury. It is sufficient that people in the past have believed such tales to be true. It is that belief that is now part of Glastonbury's own story, along with a continuing tradition of extending credulity to outlandish claims that would elsewhere be mocked.

It is infectious. On the top of the Tor, I am quickly overtaken by this fanciful image of a butter-fingered giant, scattering the contents of his sewing basket. It has sprung into my mind from I know not where, but no matter. I begin to peer down more closely at the twinkly dykes. And as I do, my imagination completely overheats and I conceive that their pattern is no longer random. Could they, I wonder, simultaneously casting myself in the role of the author of one of those best-selling religious mystery books with titles such as *Fingerprints of the Gods* or *The Sign and the Seal*, be hieroglyphs, spelling out an ancient riddle that would at a stroke solve the mystery of the true purpose of the Tor?

And why not? For on this inverted ice-cream cone's blank, tiered slopes, many an equally incredible legend has taken

You can still imagine Glastonbury Tor as an island. (© iStock)

root – that it contains in its darkest depths a lost cave which was regarded by ancient Celts as the entrance to Annwn, the underworld realm of King Gwyn; that on its peak where the ruined tower of a medieval church now stands was once the lonely, windswept early-fifth-century hermitage of Saint Patrick, scourge of snakes; or that it was the stronghold where King Melwas of the 'Summer County' (Somerset, that is, not the 1970s brand of cheap margarine) imprisoned the beautiful Guinevere until Arthur came heroically to rescue his beloved.

You can take your pick. Or make up your own. Truth in Glastonbury is so elastic and lost in the mists of time that one more theory will not do any harm. This town is up there with Stonehenge, the Pyramids and Machu Picchu as among the most projected-upon enigmas of our own and many previous ages.

The accumulation of so much legend and counter-legend is, I suppose, better suited to somewhere that doesn't exist at all – the lost city of Atlantis, or various other El Dorados that have briefly captured imaginations – but Glastonbury is real enough and the final destination on my pilgrimage, as it is on the journeys of many others. Such as Angela, a middle-aged wages clerk from Staffordshire who I met earlier this May Day morning at a celebration at the Chalice Well which sits in the folds at the foot of the Tor. She described herself as a pagan, 'but not a very devout one', and heads here on high days and holidays because Glastonbury represents for her, she had told me, a window on another world.

'There are plenty of places with pagan associations nearer to my home,' she had conceded, gathering her black cloak round her neck to keep out the 7 a.m. chill, 'and plenty elsewhere. I'm going to Avebury tomorrow as a matter of fact, but Glastonbury stands out because of its energy.' 'Energy?' I queried. 'Yes, you know. It rises up from the layers of history, one piled on top of the other.' Piled as high as the Tor, I had been tempted to joke, but kept my peace. Pagans, I have discovered on my travels, may distance themselves from many aspects of more conventional religions, but share with them an absence of a sense of humour about their spiritual beliefs.

Unlike Angela, many seekers choose to live here all the year round, which accounts for Glastonbury having, to my untrained eye, the highest concentration of holistic crystal therapists, Qigong teachers and shamanic drummers per head of the population of any British town. Its reputation also permits the forgotten pleasure of walking along a high street denuded of all the usual chain-stores, though whether the warm feeling would continue when I needed a pint of milk and couldn't find one in the tarot booths, gift emporia with names such as the Cat & Cauldron, and 'spirit' booksellers, I'm not convinced.

One of this last group of traders has a window display of an illustrated tome called *Believe Your Dreams*. It sounds like the catchphrase on a tourist advertisement for an Indian Ocean beach resort, but it might, more accurately, be used to promote Glastonbury, if further promotion is needed. The place is today so self-consciously spiritual and mysterious already that its twin town is not some plain, down-to-earth *stadt* in Germany or French *departement*, but Lalibela in Ethiopia whose extraordinary half-buried churches, hewn out of the rock by person or persons unknown hundreds if not thousands of years ago, provoke a similar quota of unanswerable questions, visiting questers and eccentric theories.

The cynical might say that Glastonbury is a caricature of itself. I can see what they are getting at, but they are missing one important thing. Despite the sort of cheerful mystical excess and guileless alternative posturing for which the town is celebrated (and which has been, by and large, unknown in the sacred places on the rest of my itinerary), there remains something wafting in the air in Glastonbury, behind the whiff of joss-sticks and the self-conscious wackiness, that is intriguing and sets you thinking afresh and in unconventional ways, not least about hidden messages spelt out by drainage ditches.

*   *   *

The early-morning mist is rising like steam off the rhynes of the Somerset Levels as I approach Glastonbury. This whole area, bordered on three sides by the Mendips and Quantocks, with the Severn Estuary on the fourth, was once regularly under water. As recently as the 1870s, whole swathes were in effect a Severn Estuary Extension between October and March. Then, with that modern determination to conquer nature, along came Victorian pumping stations and – in the twentieth century – improved coastal defences. Together they systemized the previously *ad hoc* Levels reclamation schemes that stretch back through medieval times to when the Romans were in Britain. The seasonal inland sea was drained and the surplus water channelled into ditches, controlled by clyses (sluices) and lined by willows whose new growth or withies provided the raw material for a basket-making industry that just about survives to this day.

This wholesale reordering of a natural landscape could not, however, shift the hillocks such as Glastonbury Tor, that have protruded out of the wetlands since time immemorial, but it recategorized them. For Glastonbury Tor and its near neighbour, Wearyall Hill, were both once islands. Indeed, the Isle of Avalon is still the nomenclature preferred by some to describe the environs of Glastonbury, among them the spiritually inclined who, as I have already discovered, have long had a thing about the other-worldly qualities of islands.

Trees and droves (green lanes) alongside the main road into Glastonbury from the north west manage to blot out, despite my straining neck and consequently erratic driving, the antici-pated views of the Tor. Then, just as I pass the old Clark's shoe factory at Street, it suddenly looms up on the horizon, as if from nowhere, high, proud and intimidating, filling the car windscreen. It is as if I have been floating in a small boat on a fog-bound ocean when the mist suddenly lifts to reveal us under the bow of a huge liner.

The image is an apt one because water plays such a major part in the back story of Glastonbury. It may now all be neatly channelled and drained away so as to produce decent arable

Glastonbury offers a warm welcome to outlandish claims
that would elsewhere be mocked. (© iStock)

land, but once the regular inundations by the sea left ancient Glastonbury high and dry without clean drinking water. Which is where my first stop in the town came in. For as long as there are records of Glastonbury, the Chalice Well has provided an unpolluted and bottomless source of drinking water, staving off drought in the town as recently as 1922, and supplying at various times the abbey, the church of St Michael's that, in the thirteenth century, stood atop the Tor, and the rest of the pilgrim and permanent populations. It yields its bounty of 25,000 gallons every day at an unvarying rate and temperature and, inevitably, has its own legends. Joseph of Arimathea, it is said, either buried the Holy Grail chalice here that gives the spring its name, or at the very least washed it in the waters. Some believe that the well ever after has contained traces of the blood of Christ and has miraculous healing powers, but scientists suggest the blush is a result of the presence of tiny quantities of iron.

That long association as hallowed ground led, in 1959, to the well being placed in the care of a charitable trust which is this early morning marking May Day with a celebration of

'Summer's Kindling and Nature's Growing'. As I park my car in a nearby side street, there is already a steady stream of people in through the entrance, though the street lights are still on.

The trust was set up by what sounds like an archetypal Glastonbury character, Wellesley Tudor Pole (1884–1968). He had been drawn to the town as a young man, in the early years of the twentieth century, after he experienced a vision of himself as a monk at the abbey. He was someone who claimed to live between two timescales. In the more familiar domain of the here and now, he served as a major in the army during the First World War, and in the second organized the Big Ben Silent Minute, the forerunner of the two-minute silence on the eleventh hour of the eleventh day of the eleventh month. Tudor Pole was, however, also a spiritualist, in regular contact with 'the other side' beyond the grave and able, by his own description, to cross conventional barriers of past, present and future. He was, he told the novelist Rosamond Lehmann, who developed an interest in the supernatural after the early death of her beloved daughter, 'a modest and anonymous ambassador from elsewhere'. By night he reported that he would rise from his sleep and ride off through time, calling on King Arthur and his Round Table, inventing a cure for cancer, and even, on one occasion, bumping into Jesus (though not in Glastonbury).

Next to Tudor Pole, the crowd gathering in the Cress Field, at the top end of the Chalice Well gardens, is pretty conventional. There are, admittedly, a few more full-length capes than you usually see at your local bus stop, but nothing like the cascade of them I had witnessed at Stonehenge. The central flat arena of the field is flanked by terraced slopes where fellow May Day celebrants are beginning to fill up the natural pews. As I make my way towards a gap where I can plonk down on my plastic bag (vital protection against the heavy dew still on the ground), I spot a few familiar faces from Stonehenge. The woman who had worn a lop-sided daisy on her forehead there is today more in bud than bloom, with a pale green full-length skirt and a simple garland of spring flowers in her blonde hair. Others have opted for a more practical fleece, shawl or rug – in one case a Burberry blanket – against the chill, but the halo of flowers appears to be the must-have item for this ceremony. Male pagans are clearly and commendably more in touch with their feminine side than the rest of the men in the population.

I have celebrated May Day morning by getting up with the dawn only once before, and that was many moons ago when I was a student. As I watch people arrive in the Cress Field, trying not to notice the damp creeping into the seat of my trousers, I find that I cannot now recall anything else about the traditional May Morning assembly on Magdalen Bridge in Oxford other than the choristers singing from the top of a college tower, and the foolish jumping into the River Cherwell below and landing, like human punt poles, in the mud that lay no more than 18 inches under the water. Were there ambulances on hand to take them to a spinal injuries unit?

I had gone because I had been told that every student did. In that sense I'd followed the crowd. My fellow worshippers this morning are doing the opposite – going against the crowd. Pagans (or to be more correct, neo-pagans; given the largely successful campaign of Western Christianity to persecute paganism out of existence, this is technically and demonstrably reborn paganism, rather than an unbroken line with pre-Inquisition Jesus refusniks) remain a tiny minority in the general population, and moreover, one that is regarded with a certain distrust. Even, it seems, in pagan-friendly Glastonbury. Beyond the Chalice Well's boundaries stands a tall, cream-painted house with a terrace in front. The noise has brought a youngish woman outside in her dressing gown, looking a bit like Cherie Blair when she famously got out of bed to open the front door of her Islington home on 2 May 1997 to take delivery of a bunch of flowers. She leans on the railings and peers over grumpily at the assembly in the Cress Field, scowls when I try to meet her eye with a smile, and then disappears inside.

The May Day festivities mark the mid-point between the

spring equinox and the summer solstice in traditional calendars dictated by solar and lunar movements. Beltane – May Day – is one of four cross quarter days. Imbolc (February), Beltane, Lughnasa (August) and Samhain (November) are found in ancient Gaelic and Celtic rites, disappeared with the arrival of Christianity when their place in the calendar was usurped by saints' days, but have been revived in recent times.

Beltane in particular is popular because it is ripe with promise, the start of the summer pastoral season, when the sap is rising. All very Freudian. It has been adapted subsequently by many usurpers – from the church festivals that mark 1 May as the start of the month of the Virgin Mary in Catholic nations, to its designation by the international trade union movement as a day for workers and a public holiday in some European countries. So while in Glastonbury we are witnessing the lighting of one of two Beltane fires in the Cress Field, in France, as I have been hearing on the car radio on the journey down, disgruntled employees are taking to the streets of major cities to demand changes in economic and labour policy.

The small, low-lying Beltane fire, tended by a young man in a poncho, is now ablaze, symbolically banishing winter darkness, but the bigger of the two pyres, branches arranged like a wigwam and decorated with May blossom, lies as yet untouched. The late arrivals are still scrambling up the slopes to find seats. There must be around 250 of us gathered. 'It is good fortune to lick the morning dew,' remarks Uta sitting next to me. At first I think she is inviting me to join her in a pagan ritual, but then she points, by way of explanation, at a teenager slipping down the slope on her face. Uta hails from Germany, she says, but came to live in Glastonbury 20 years back 'because it is at the centre'.

Drummers are gathering round the smaller fire to warm the skins of their hand-held instruments. They then take up positions and begin to beat out a welcome. As the sun slowly climbs in the sky, illuminating the Tor that is just visible through the silver birch and willow trees, two women – one older and slightly lost in a voluminous green and silver sleeping bag coat, the other younger and sporting a close-fitting brown velvet jacket and ankle-length brown, gold and pink striped skirt – step forward to cheers and applause.

'Can you feel the life force rising from the earth?' one begins. More cheers. 'Let's connect with that energy. Let's feel at one with Mother Earth. Let's draw it into ourselves. Let's honour oneness and connection with all things.' As she speaks, I wonder out loud to Uta how to describe this woman – priest, leader, facilitator? 'No words,' she says, smiling but shaking her head. 'We are democratic.'

The second woman is now squatting next to the unlit fire. 'Close your eyes,' she demands. 'Look with your inner eye. Feel presence in this sacred place. Feel the energy rising.' The drummers hoik up the volume. 'Send roots down,' she shouts over them, 'into the earth, into the darkness, into the beautiful, damp, fertile earth. Squat and touch it.'

It is quite a feat to keep your balance on the narrow ledges of the slope, but most follow her instructions. 'Feel right down to the fire, to the molten rock, to the fire of life,' she goes on. 'And now start to draw it up, draw it into you. Feel it coursing through your bodies.' Her eyes are closed and her face is creased in concentration, like paper that has been crumpled and smoothed out again. All around the Cress Field people start calling out in pleasure, whooping and clapping.

As befits this outdoor place of worship, the ceremony is informal, a series of crescendos and lulls. Our leaders – I can't think of a better word – allow plenty of whooping space round each section. So, after a suitable pause for discussion (Uta is now avoiding my gaze, disapproving, I suspect, because I have so far remained firmly on my wet backside), there is another salvo of drums to refocus attention. It is the start of a chant. 'I am the walking breath, I am the spirit of earth. I am alive and walking, where I am is beautiful.'

It begins with a handful of voices and steadily builds. Those who have instruments – one man is blowing into the mid-point of what looks like a long twig – take them up, and those confident enough to add a descant do so. The noise level rises quickly, and as it does people go into the centre to join hands in a spiral round and round the larger fire. A few leap up at once, but most are slower to venture forward. The combination of the beat of the music, the chorus of the chant, and the stamping of feet on the ground as the circle winds round and round and round, is sending out magnetic waves. It's impossible to resist.

I take my place between a teenage boy in chain mail and what I realize too late is his girlfriend, her hair jet black, and her face punctuated with studs. There is no time or gap in the swelling sound for introductions, but they seem unperturbed by my intrusion. The real joy being generated by this crowd is palpable. It reminds me of ceilidhs I've been to at Irish country weddings, ice-breakers where strangers from different extremes of the bride's and groom's families who otherwise would have no contact are thrown together, hand in hand, and in that instant become good friends.

When the slopes of the Cress Field are all but bare and the concentric rings can hardly squeeze in without tipping the front row onto the fire, the drums bring the chanting to a peak. More whooping and hugging. Feet, called into action, seem unwilling to be still. It is time, as the man in the poncho steps purposefully into the melée, to light the fire, to offer up intentions to Mother Earth 'and the faeries from this magical vale who are joining us'.

The floor is open for anyone to add their intentions. 'Our ancestors,' calls out one voice behind me. 'Planet earth,' chips in another. 'Avalon,' shouts the girl next to me. That raises a big cheer. 'The bees.' More cheers. 'Eco-affluence.' That is greeted with the sort of 'wooow' that you usually hear in response to an acid put-down by Lily Savage.

The list goes on and on, but the themes are quickly established. As the flames take hold, we eventually fall into silence, eyes all turned to the warmth. There is none of the fear usually associated with fire, just a sort of fascination as the may boughs catch alight. The only noise is now the crackling and spitting of the fire.

The spell lasts for a minute or two but then is broken by an announcement. It is time to jump the Beltane fire, 'to leave all that separates us behind and jump into the one'. For health and safety reasons, it is going to have to be the smaller of the two blazes which has been built specially for the purpose. The chanting starts up again and, with no apparent organization but great precision, the spiral slowly unravels itself. The front row duck through an arch of hands and then wend their way between each existing ring of the circle, dragging others behind them, until everyone emerges at the other end.

The queue for Beltane fire-jumping is long. I leave it to the last minute to join, watching the pioneers so as to get my technique right. They come in pairs and threes. Some leap, others do an exaggerated skip. Those in long skirts bunch them up at their waists. All the time they are cheered on by onlookers. One older lady in purple even manages it with her walking stick, but then a German visitor trips and collapses on landing. After a brief hiatus, she is helped away to a first-aid tent. The music continues throughout this mini-drama, and everyone waits their turn good-humouredly, chanting, singing or talking excitedly. On either side of me, two women dance rhythmically, arms extended then brought down by their sides and up again, like the figures on the spinning cylinder in the opening credits of television's *Tales of the Unexpected*.

By the time I reach the front of the queue, the focus is already moving to the maypole, so I do it largely unobserved. I skip over the embers, the sensation of heat around my ankles there for a moment. A single figure is all that is left of the crowd on the other side, but she grins, shakes a small pole with bells and pats me on the back as I land.

Am I cleansed? No, but the sense of having taken part in a communal activity that has clearly meant so much to others is tangible. Participating rather than observing, being open rather than closed, putting to one side the contemporary concerns of looking foolish, everything having a point or purpose is strangely liberating.

The women have begun processing down through the

gardens to a lower lawn to prepare themselves to crown the maypole – to be carried to them by the men – with a ring of may flowers. This is all explained by the woman in the brown velvet jacket with a none-too-subtle nod in the direction of its nudge-nudge-wink-wink connotations. A long, slender pole is already being held shoulder-high by a group of men gathered in the centre of the Cress Field. There is no room for extra bodies and pairs of hands, so the rest of us fall in behind, chanting, 'Tree of life growing higher, dragon rising from the Beltane fire' and head off to circle a row of yew trees three times before joining up with the women.

As we pass the Chalice Well itself, encased since the twelfth century in a shaft said to be built with stones rescued from Glastonbury Abbey after it burned down in 1184, the man next to me, in his early thirties and dishevelled in a brown-and-black monk's outfit, breaks off from the chanting. 'It feels like stepping into Doctor Who's tardis being here, doesn't it?' he remarks. It hadn't quite struck me that way. 'You know, going back in time, back to where it all started.' John had first been 'dragged here', he reports, in 1993 when still a student. 'I'm not a pagan or anything. I only came because it was too hard to say no.' 'You don't sound like you're taking it very seriously,' I say. He looks surprised. 'Oh, I do. I am. That's why I still keep coming. It explains so much.'

There is no chance to pin down quite what is being explained by what is seeming increasingly like a party game. The pole is crowned, planted in its stand on the lower lawn and hauled upright. Red and white ribbons hang down from the top. As the music starts up, individuals, couples and groups grab hold of the ends and start weaving in and out of each other.

I retreat to a paved platform behind a flower bed to take in the whole spectacle. On one side of me, a young man with a hemp peasant's smock over his 'normal clothes' is standing like a statue, head back, arms spread out at his side and legs apart, as if he is sunbathing while standing up. It would be rude to interrupt. On the other side is the fire jumper with the stick.

Tall and very erect, she introduces herself as Mary. What brings her here today? 'It is a special anniversary for me,' she confides. 'I've been out of the convent as long as I was in it.' It isn't what I'd expected. How long? 'Twenty-five years in, and now twenty-five years out.' She has travelled down from London with a friend, another ex-nun. How do they accommodate today's rituals with their Christianity? 'Oh, we don't.' She laughs. 'This is where it all comes from. Christianity is just something that has been put on top of this. I realized that a long time ago. This is much more real.'

The vocabulary – 'real', explaining unnamed things, feeling energy – is impenetrable. Shifts of dancers have by now wrapped the red and white ribbons all the way down the pole. People are gathering round, hands reaching over shoulders to touch the pole. 'We're going to end with a meditation,' our leader announces, beating on her drum. The crowd falls half-silent. The group round the pole bend in, as if all pushing from their opposite and equal sides. Slowly a chant of 'uuummm' goes up. 'They're radiating out their energy,' Mary explains.

*   *   *

The closely cropped lawns around the ruins of Glastonbury Abbey are – by contrast with the exuberant party I've just left behind at the Chalice Well – empty and very still. No celebrations, no mention of Beltane, no loose vocabulary being bandied around, and certainly no exuberance, though a member of staff (it has been run as a trust since 1907) dressed as a serving wench is trying to entice the only other visitors, a group of schoolchildren in blazers and ties, into the 'living museum' in what was once the abbot's kitchen.

The remnants of the abbey – built on a breathtaking scale in 1184 and destroyed in a breaktaking rage by Henry VIII (the elderly last abbot, Richard Whiting, was hanged, drawn and quartered atop the Tor) – suggest the sort of dramatic, bloody but familiar story of English Reformation history that has been a part of most of the places I have so far visited. It therefore hardly fits with the rest of Glastonbury's trademark alternative way of seeing and doing things. This abbey may have been celebrated – the Domesday Book reports in 1086 that it, or its immediate precursor, was the richest in the land with £840 per year – and regularly frequented by royals, but it is part of the mainstream institutional Christian tale of Britain that has left our landscape dotted with many a similar ruin.

However, on closer inspection, what remains of the abbey soon offers up its own peculiar monuments to the layers of local folklore. First, marked out with such discrete edging stones in what was once the Choir of the abbey that it might just be a place to put bins or park buggies, I stumble across the tomb of Arthur and Guinevere. Again their names have already come up in other places I have visited. Some historians dispute that Arthur ever existed. There is no mention of him, they note, in the *Anglo-Saxon Chronicles*, one of the principal sources for what were allegedly his times. Others maintain, though, that he was a warrior king who led the Britons in battle against the Saxons and died around 539. The trappings of his legend, his sword Excalibur, his Knights, the Round Table, Camelot, Merlin and so forth, appear mainly to have come from the imagination of the twelfth-century historian, Geoffrey of Monmouth and his *History of the Kings of Britain* (1138).

This is, as I discovered at Stonehenge, a fanciful work that fuses myth with history. Whether Geoffrey made up the heroic tale of Arthur, embroidered on an existing oral tradition, or based it on details that were available to him but are now lost to us, is hotly debated, but somehow the dispute feels utterly irrelevant this May morning. The fact is that the legend took hold and carried Glastonbury in its wake. It became the staple of romantic literature of the medieval period, and because people have wanted it to be true, for whatever reasons of their own, it has survived, with peaks and troughs, until today. The focus for much of that yearning has been Glastonbury.

Just over half a century after Geoffrey of Monmouth first wrote of Arthur, his legend was given a huge boost by the 'discovery' in 1191 of the tombs of the warrior king and his queen, Guinevere, within Glastonbury Abbey. Following a prophecy, the monks, according to the contemporary chroni- cler Gerald of Wales, had dug into the walls of the abbey and found a hollowed-out oak. 'Within it lay two skeletons, one male, one female. A lock of golden hair still clung to the woman's skull; the man, tall and broad, had ten wounds to his head. And buried with them was a lead cross inscribed, "Here lies the renowned king Arthur with Guinevere his second wife in the Isle of Avalon".'

The discovery made Glastonbury one of the pre-eminent places of pilgrimage in Britain. By 1278, the site where Arthur had been disinterred was so celebrated that King Edward I and his wife, Eleanor of Castile, came to the abbey to witness the relics being placed in a black marble tomb on the high altar. The carefully delineated rectangle of grass in the ruins before me marks the spot where that monument stood until the Dis- solution.

Again what is important for this story of pilgrimage is that those who came were convinced that these were the bones of Arthur and Guinevere, and they invested that conviction in Glastonbury, but it is hard not to suspect the motives of the abbey monks. Just seven years before the 'discovery', a fire had destroyed the abbey and the community was busy fund-raising to build another. Linking that appeal with such a spectacular find would have made good commercial sense in an age when relics were big business. And link it they clearly did. In the fourteenth century, pilgrim numbers and donations placed Glastonbury second only to Westminster Abbey in terms of the wealth of individual monasteries.

There have been three abbeys in total on this site. Two are well documented. There was the one destroyed by fire, which had its origins in Saxon Christianity, and the patronage of King Ine of Wessex in the early eighth century. It was subse- quently added to by Abbot Dunstan in the tenth century before he went off to become Archbishop of Canterbury, and then by the Normans after the Conquest in 1066 as part of their efforts to bend the Church to their will. And after the fire, there was the new building that rose from the ashes, helped by the money of pilgrims coming to see Arthur's bones; this lasted with its roof on until the Reformation, and is a ruin to this day.

The third – and earliest – incarnation requires more of a leap of faith and imagination. If the legend of Arthur and his Avalon is linked with the abbey site, so too is that of Jesus visiting the town. For the ruined abbey stands on the site of the 'Old Church', reputedly built here from mud and wood by Jesus himself as a tribute to his mother when he was passing through some time around the year 20. This story makes the claim on the information board as I walked into the abbey grounds – 'The cradle of Christianity in England' – sound an extraordinary understatement. If it is true that Jesus was here, then this is one of the birthplaces of global Christianity.

If the tale is true . . . how quickly Glastonbury is working its romance on me as I pick my way through the layers. An old church did, it seems, exist, though every last substantial trace of it was destroyed in the great fire of 1184. Did Jesus come and build it? Well, that prompts two questions. The son of a poor carpenter from Nazareth may have been easily capable of building a church, using skills learnt at his father's knee, but would an individual from backward, introspective Galilee – 'Can anything good come from that place?' someone remarks in horror in John's Gospel – really be likely to go on an extended gap year before getting on with his public ministry? And, even if he was, why would he have chosen Glastonbury? 'Because of its energy', 'Because it is at the centre'. I can hear the voices of my fellow pilgrims echoing unconvincingly in my ears.

Amid the shelf-loads of religious mystery literature which has proved to be such a commercial success in recent times, there is a strain that likes nothing better than filling in the gaps in the Gospels. So because Jesus's life from age six months to 30 is a blank, this school insists on making something up to fill in that space. Miles Kington once parodied the approach on Channel 4 with his programme *In Search of the Holy Foreskin*.

And this strain in the same overall field attempts to make improbable connections between folklorish myths and ancient landmarks to 'reveal' *sub rosa* civilizations. Put the two together, and it is somehow inevitable that there are those who have attempted to mount a 'factually based' case to prove that Jesus's feet did, in ancient times, walk upon England's mountains green, or to be more precise, hillocks such as Glastonbury Tor.

Again, the thing to note is not how threadbare such books are, but that people want to read them. And then to ask, 'Why?' I jot down a list of possibilities on the back of my Glastonbury Abbey guidebook as I sit on a bench, with the cider orchard behind me (what is it with monks and cider?) and the ruined nave standing aloof in front: (1) Because the traditional Christian story, the chronology of ecclesiastical history in these lands, is so well known and still such a source of division between the denominations, that people simply want another variation on the religious theme? (2) Supplementary to one – because such books chime with an instinctive suspicion of the prescribed, authorized version of our religious past produced by what can sometimes feel like the clerical/academic police? (3) A consequence of number two – because there are plenty of conspiracy theorists out there who like the idea of God but distrust organized religion because they feel that it misrepresents its own past?

There is probably an element of truth in all of the above, but there is also the sense that such unorthodox research and improvable theories dovetail with the spiritual exploration going on beyond the reach of facts, institutions and denominations. For they offer a version of religion that is essentially flexible. In Glastonbury, you are presented with a selection of ancient legends, all of which speak through the landscape of the town, and then you are free – indeed encouraged – to shape them into anything that takes your fancy. Everything is valid because everything is subjective.

There is one more piece to the puzzle-that-has-no-solution in the grounds of the abbey – a small thorn tree. It is tucked away behind the visitor centre and I am about to walk out of the exit when I belatedly spot it. One of a number of 'holy thorns' dotted about Glastonbury – there is one on the top of Wearyall Hill, another in the churchyard of St John's parish church, and one in the Chalice Well gardens – this tree is part of a horticultural apostolic succession that dates back to the visit of Joseph of Arimathea around AD 63. When he got out of his boat and set foot on Wearyall Island, as it was then, he rested briefly on his wooden stick, pressing it into the ground, where it took root in the soil. Another version suggests that Joseph brought with him one of the thorns from the crown placed on Jesus's head at the crucifixion and planted it in Glastonbury's miraculous soil where it quickly blossomed. From that original has been grown every tree since, including the abbey's current incumbent, planted in 1992 after its 80-year-old predecessor withered and died. To add lustre to the legend, the tree in question – and what are presumably cuttings from it – blooms twice a year, at Easter and at Christmas. And the species is unknown elsewhere in Britain. Its natural home is the Middle East.

The high point of interest in the Joseph of Arimathea story came in the late fifteenth/early sixteenth century when a chapel of St Joseph was dedicated at the abbey. Perhaps interest in Arthur's tomb had waned and this was by way of a new attraction. Even the Reformation failed to stop the cult of the thorn tree. In January 1753, *Gentleman's Magazine* reported from Glastonbury: 'A vast concourse of people attended the noted thorn on Christmas-day, new style; but, to their great disappointment, there was no appearance of its blowing, which made them watch it narrowly the 5th of January, the Christmas-day, old style, when it blowed as usual.'

*   *   *

The May sunshine is giving way to clouds, and my darning needles are now unmistakeably drainage ditches. The real world is calling. I take my leave of the top of the Tor, past boxes of plastic cups and candles that have been left behind by early-morning revellers. On the gentler of the two paths down, I am trying to remember exactly what it is I have read about the convergence of ley-lines on Glastonbury, when it comes back to me that the consensus is that no such things exist. Perhaps I am still a little bit in Glastonbury's thrall, because I decide that even if they don't, they should. For if these supposed conductors of mystical and psychic energy did intersect in this Somerset town, they would bring me back to T. S. Eliot's verse-line about 'the intersection of the timeless moment' with which this whole journey began. They might also provide a handy metaphor for tying up the various threads of my pilgrimage.

In its willingness to be all things to all comers, Glastonbury contains an overlap with each of the other seven stories I have told. There are its Arthurian connections, shared with Stonehenge and Bardsey; the all-too-visible pagan roots showing through subsequent attempts to Christianize customs here, as in the well-dressings of Derbyshire; its history of being that mythical place, the island, just like Lindisfarne, Bardsey and Iona; its tales of healing, shared with Holywell and Walsingham; its place in the tale of the Celtic saints thanks to Patrick; and in the evolution from Celtic worship to Anglo-Saxon Christianity to rule from Rome to Henry VIII's national Church.

A pilgrimage is in one way following a line from place to place, placing one foot in front of another. It is also, I realize, about coming round in a circle. Here at Glastonbury, that circle is closing. Glastonbury arguably does everything any of the other sacred spots do, only much more flamboyantly. It welcomes and accommodates with gusto all comers – the weirder their take, the better. It stands out more obviously against the logic of the commercial world. But its core story is the same as I have found elsewhere, one all about being a beacon for spiritual searchers who take their cue from its past, and who are coming in increasing numbers, many of them having tired of the great institutions of religion, or, among the

Ley-lines are reputed to converge on Glastonbury
and its Tor (© iStock)

younger May Day fire-jumpers, having rejected them out of
hand.

This is, I believe, a compelling story that turns on its head
the conventional wisdom that Britain is now a country
without religion. What has taken place is that, along with
everything else these past three decades, religion has been
privatized. It happens now not exclusively in houses of God,
but in the heads and hearts of those who continue to seek,
some of them by travelling to holy places where they discern
the wisdom and example of the past, and find in it a way
through the present. Such an approach is almost impossible
for statisticians to quantify. Imagine standing at the Chalice
Well, where the party is still going on by the sound of things,

with a clipboard and trying to persuade each individual to put a label on their beliefs.

If I were a bishop or archbishop, I might find this a dispiriting conclusion for the future of my institution, but as a fellow seeker I have grown to appreciate the emotion, the independence, the democracy and the innovation of those I have encountered in these far-flung sacred spots. Perhaps these are examples that the institutions of faith could learn from.

So where does that leave my own spiritual search? Ongoing, I think would be a good word, though not perhaps at the intensity of the past eleven months. Going to Bardsey prompted me to pick up a volume of R. S. Thomas's collected poems. On the long trek back from Iona, I found the following, which just about sums up what has changed – or not – in me. It comes at the end of a poem called 'Counterpoint':

> I think that maybe
> I will be a little surer
> Of being a little nearer.
> That's all. Eternity
> Is in the understanding
> That that little is more than enough.

Acknowledgements

My thanks, above all, go to those I met at the eight locations featured in the book for sharing their thoughts and experiences with me. Those who agreed to be quoted have been identified. Others – because they wanted their names held back, or because our encounters were too brief to seek consent – have been given other names.

The following have all played a much appreciated role in helping me bring this idea to fruition: Lynne Bagshaw, Robin Baird-Smith, Caroline Chartres, Dr Liz Cole-Hamilton, Pete Coppola, Lucinda Coxon, Kevin Crossley-Holland, the Revd Evelyn Davies, Carol Dougall, Margiad Eckstein, Pam Etherington-Smith, Fiona Fraser, Fr Gregory Hallam, the Revd Nick Hawkins, Gwen Herbert, Derek Johns, Sara Maitland, Maggie Mason and Bill and Monica White.

And my biggest debt, as ever, is to my children, Kit and Orla, and to my wife, Siobhan, for never complaining when I was away, and encouraging me to write it all down when I was home.